A Love and a Grief so Deep

by Marlene Anderson

Printed in the United States of America

ISBN 978-1-60266-660-3

All rights reserved solely by the author. The author guarantees all contents are original and do not infringe upon the legal rights of any other person or work. No part of this book may be reproduced in any form without the permission of the author. The views expressed in this book are not necessarily those of the publisher.

Unless otherwise indicated, Bible quotations are taken from The New Oxford Annotated version of the Bible, revised standard version, edited by Herbert G. May and Bruce M. Metzger. Copyright © 1962, 1973 by Oxford University Press, Inc., New York

The Message, the Bible in contemporary language by Eugene H. Peterson, p. 1085, NavPress, 2002

www.xulonpress.com

Table of Contents

Chapter 1	The Ticking Clock	11
Chapter 2	Shock and Disbelief	19
Chapter 3	From Crisis to Crisis	25
Chapter 4	Denial	35
Chapter 5	A Reprieve	39
Chapter 6	Fear Returns	45
Chapter 7	A Hope and Spirit Tested	51
Chapter 8	The Downward Slide	57
Chapter 9	Walking Through the Valley	67
Chapter 10	Walking Alone	77
Chapter 11	Details and More Details	83
Chapter 12	A Grief so Deep	89
Chapter 13	Music and More Music	95
Chapter 14	Memories	101
Chapter 15	Another Crisis - Another Struggle	107
Chapter 16	Emerging from the Valley	113

Dedication

 *T*his book is dedicated to Le Roy, a man of great talents and abilities who enriched the lives of so many people. I am proud to have been a part of that life.

 It is also dedicated to all our friends who loved us, helped us through the journey from crisis to death, and comforted and supported me continually after his death. We could not have made it without your help. Thank you for your friendship and love.

 And to my children: Bob, Elizabeth and Don. You are the love of my life.

PART ONE

THE JOURNEY BEGINS

Chapter 1

The Ticking Clock

I am stunned. It can't be true. Le Roy is the healthiest man I know. He is never sick. A brain tumor? Impossible! The only time he has gone to the hospital is when he is visiting me or his mom. There must be some mistake!

That was my reaction to hearing Le Roy had a brain tumor. From the first words of his primary care physician, "It doesn't look good," to the week after when we learned it was inoperable, our life as we knew it had ended. Although my brain cried, "No, it can't be true," it was true.

And so began our journey from crisis to crisis and eventually death. I had fallen into some crack in the earth where everything is upside down and inside out and a crazy rabbit runs around with a large ticking clock saying, "I'm late – I'm late," because his time was running out.

Time was running out. Inside Le Roy's head was a mass of wild cells that were taking control of his intelligent and wonderful brain. As I tried to grasp what the doctor was telling us, it was like watching some horror movie where this glutinous thing comes creeping along, covering and destroying everything in its path. Only these were his own cells that had gone amuck. How could we get rid of them before it was too late? There must be a way. Surgery – chemo – radiation – there had to be a solution.

My head was spinning as were our lives. I needed to find a way to stop and get off this crazy ride that was moving faster and faster. Life was spinning out of control. And we walked out of the doctor's office in a daze.

On January 29, 2001 we discovered that the symptoms we were beginning to see of a man out of touch with time and unable to process time was the result of an aggressive brain tumor. Somewhere in those first few days, I picked up my pen and started journaling. It was the only way I knew to keep my sanity. And it was where I found God waiting for me.

So early every morning while my husband slept, drugged on medications to keep him from having seizures, I picked up my Bible along with pencil and paper, and started randomly reading. I had been a student of the Bible for many years. I had attended Bible Study Fellowship, taught Sunday school, and even put together class curriculum for the eighth and ninth graders that I taught in my church. Now I held a new Bible, called "The Message" that I heard such wonderful comments about. From the very first, it was as though God was directing the pages to fall open to what He wanted me to hear that would give me the support and comfort I needed for that day. Passages seemed to literally jump off the page at me.

My Journal:
"Do not fear; only believe and she [he] shall be well." (Luke 8:50) This is a journey of faith and hope we are on, and where it is taking us I don't know. I just know we have to put our trust in God. Every morning, now, it seems God is reaching out to me and giving me the passages I need to hear, and I am hanging on to them for dear life. Fear has a stronghold. Yet, fear has no power – fear can be conquered. I am going to put my trust in what God says to me every morning.

"And I tell you, Ask and it will be given you; seek, and you will find; knock, and it will be opened to you. For every one who asks receives, and he who seeks finds, and to him who knocks it will be opened. What father among you, if his son asks for a fish, will instead of a fish give him a serpent; or if he asks for an egg, will give him *a scorpion? If you then, who are evil, know how to give good gifts to your children, how much more will the heavenly Father give the Holy Spirit to those who ask him!" (Luke 11:9-13)*

Was God telling me, that if I trust enough, things will turn out okay? I so longed to believe that. Yet I knew that the passage wasn't speaking of miracles happening just because you asked for one. But I knew that God would give me His Holy Spirit to lead and guide me through this maze and tangle of heightened emotions.

It was in those few moments each morning that I gathered the strength I needed to meet the crisis that challenged me that day. After we received that first diagnosis, it seemed that not only had the world speeded up to breakneck speed, but the decisions required demanded instantaneous thought and wisdom. And they were life and death decisions. We had begun a race; the race of a lifetime that would end four months later with my husband's death. But in the beginning it was a race we believed we might be able to win.

We weren't sure when this silent killer began its invasion of Le Roy's brain. Some of the doctors felt the tumor had started rapidly within the last few months, while others thought it might have started slowly over the course of a year and then escalated in December. What we did know is that it began to grow on the right side of the frontal lobe and that is where the largest growth was. Because the frontal lobes of both sides of the brain are similar, the left side was compensating in thinking and processing daily information while the tumor was growing on the right side. Symptoms didn't really become apparent until the tumor began wrapping itself around the corpus callosum, the large group of nerves that separate the two halves of the brain, and then crossed to the left side.

Were there any telltale signs of this impending crisis? In retrospect there might have been, but at the time they just seemed like things you might see happening with normal aging: Le Roy was becoming a little slower with his responses; his thinking wasn't quite as quick; there were a few headaches but nothing significant. Most of these "symptoms" began to gradually appear in December. Le Roy had just celebrated his birthday in August. He looked, felt and acted like a person twenty years younger than he was. He had no heart problems or high cholesterol, no high blood pressure or diabetes or any of the other ailments one begins to associate with the aging process. He exercised, was physically fit and had a good positive outlook on life.

On his birthday he said to a friend, "If I never live another year, I will have done everything I wanted to do." How prophetic. And there was another prophetic utterance that day – from me – although I didn't know it at the time. We had decided to play a little joke on our friends who were coming over to our house to help celebrate his birthday. While people were arriving, Le Roy was in the bedroom with our son-in-law putting ashes all over his face, arms and hair, and getting dressed like a crotchety old man, with buttons incorrectly buttoned, and a tie and shirt that clashed. Just before he made his entrance, pushed out in a wheelchair by our son-in-law, I announced his arrival to our guests with these words, "As you know, Le Roy is celebrating his 70th birthday and he neither looks nor acts like a 70 year old. *But something happens when you turn 70.*" I remember experiencing a sudden chill of fear when I said that last line and wanted immediately to take it back and say something else, but then, just as quickly, dismissed it. But later, after Le Roy's tumor had been discovered, I remembered my words and the words Le Roy spoke to our friend. Were these signs? Should we have suspected anything?

On Christmas Eve Le Roy had what appeared to be a bad flu with a severe headache and vomiting. It was usual for him to have some head congestion and a low-grade headache when he had the flu, but I couldn't remember a time when his head hurt that much, and he rarely threw up. When he was sick he just wanted to be left alone to rest until he felt better. He did not want anybody fussing over him. And, after a day or two, he was feeling better and ready to lead his band for the New Years Eve celebration at our community's clubhouse and I didn't think any more about it.

Other events took our minds off anything that might have been symptomatic with Le Roy. Our daughter Elizabeth at the age of 39 was expecting her first baby. Because of her age, she was experiencing gestational problems such as high blood pressure and diabetes and began having false labor pains in late December although the baby wasn't due until the first week in February. We were all concerned about her health and her baby because her first pregnancy had ended in a miscarriage. When she gave birth three weeks premature on January 14th to a beautiful, healthy baby girl we were all thankful. Later we would recognize just what a blessing it had been because if she had been born on her due date in February, it would have happened the same time her dad was in the hospital getting a tumor biopsy.

For Le Roy, some listlessness and fatigue was part of recovering from the flu, along with some sinus congestion, maybe a low-grade headache and sometimes a cough. We saw similar signs occurring in Le Roy this January and attributed those signs to recovery. So while there had been little signs that something wasn't quite right, they weren't out of the ordinary, and with our concerns for Elizabeth, we had little time to think about it.

It wasn't until after our daughter's baby was born that Le Roy's symptoms became more apparent and suddenly alarming. But by then the tumor was invading the left side of his brain. One day when I went to Seattle to help my daughter, I returned to find Le Roy still in his bathrobe. I was surprised and asked if he was okay. He grinned sheepishly and said yes, he was just feeling lazy. Even though a small trickle of fear was beginning deep inside me, his justification was plausible. Being retired it was normal for us not to have any major projects or do anything special during January and we would often just be lazy.

In November when he had seen his doctor for a checkup, he was told his blood pressure had risen slightly for the first time in his life. His physician was going to "watch" it to see if it got worse and suggested that our infrequent trips to the gym might be part of the problem.

So the week before he was diagnosed we made a decision to go back to the gym and start seriously exercising again. That's when the "signs" became disturbing. When we exercised, we usually began our routine on the treadmill and then finished it with specific machines. I spent less time on the treadmill and more time on the other workout machines. Le Roy, however, liked to "walk" several miles on the treadmill.

As was my habit when I finished my exercise routine first, I would go run some errands or shop for groceries and then return to pick up Le Roy. Usually he would be ready to go. But now when I returned he was still working out. The first time this happened I was a little surprised and annoyed. The second time I returned he was in the locker room. I waited and waited for him to come out, and finally, becoming alarmed, asked one of the trainers to see if he was still there. He was. Unknown to both of us the tumor was already making it impossible for Le Roy to respond to time issues. He might start something but no longer knew when to stop. The third day that week when I returned, I saw him casually going through the gym clothes for sale. When I told him it was time to go, he said he still had more exercises to do. I was confused, concerned and getting upset. This wasn't like Le Roy at all. He was always diligent about time, punctual and cooperative. I had to insist that we leave.

Something wasn't right. But what? When I questioned him, he couldn't explain it. And the nagging fear continued to build within me. At home it was more difficult to see these new differences in Le Roy.

The following Sunday, Super Bowl Sunday, I mentioned my concerns to Elizabeth and her husband Gene. I remember saying that I was beginning to think he might have suffered a little stroke at Christmas time instead of just having the flu. I even said, "It's almost as though he has a brain tumor or something," never for a minute actually believing that could be so. The kids also had noticed some changes in his personality. He just wasn't acting "quite like Dad." And at times his behavior didn't make sense. We all agreed that he needed to see his doctor as soon as possible, even though he had just seen him less than two weeks before to see if his blood pressure had gotten worse. It hadn't.

On January 29, 2001, we called the doctor's office and scheduled an emergency visit. His doctor was surprised to see us, but he listened carefully as I tried to explain our concerns. The symptoms seemed so hard to define, and yet they were so ominous. How could I explain my deep sense of alarm? It seemed as though Le Roy's personality had suddenly become blunted with a flattened affect. Yet he still seemed to be functioning quite well. But he didn't seem to have a sense of time urgency anymore, and for a professional musician that was the most "telling." The indicators were subtle, but were there. He seemed to be responding to life more by habit or rote and at times was almost in a dream-like state. He would start something and not want to stop.

His doctor asked him if he knew why his family was concerned or if he felt sick or had been depressed. Le Roy simply said no. He didn't recognize any of these symptoms within himself. After completing some routine reflexive tests, his doctor decided to schedule a CT scan just to be sure there was no reason for concern. His comment to me: "I wouldn't worry. Ninety-eight percent of the time, the scan comes back positive." This was Monday. We scheduled the CT scan for Wednesday because Le Roy was giving a music lesson on Tuesday. Even though the tumor was already quickly taking control of his brain, he was still able to teach a music lesson.

Chapter 2

Shock and Disbelief

That day I sent the first of many e-mails to close friends who were wintering in Arizona.

I have a prayer request for you. Le Roy has been having low-grade headaches since he had the flu on Christmas Eve and is scheduled for a CT scan on Wednesday. Would you please pray that if there is something to be concerned about, such as a tumor, that it would show up? And if there isn't a reason to be concerned, pray that the CT scan will show nothing and we will know that this is just an extension of the flu. No concern. Just prevention. Love to all four of you. Marlene

After the CT scan on Wednesday, we returned to hear a shocked doctor confirm my worst fear: "It doesn't look good. He has a brain tumor and it is quite large." He ordered 4 mg of Decadron to be given every six hours to prevent seizures, along with 300 mg of Dilantin, and Zantac to prevent stomach problems from the medication. My first thought was getting Le Roy to the best brain specialist in the state, which would have been in Seattle. But his doctor knew that would take time; and time was of the utmost urgency. He knew he could get him in to see a local neurosurgeon right away. A quick phone call insured an appointment the following day with a neurosurgeon in Bellingham at five P.M.

The race was on.

I don't know how much of this registered emotionally with Le Roy as we left the doctor's office, but I know I was numb with shock. Le Roy was never one to talk about his feelings. I know he understood, but I don't know how much of an emotional response his tumor allowed his brain to feel.

It was with a heavy heart that night when I called each of our kids and told them what was happening and then sent an e-mail updating my friends and asking for prayers. I was very scared.

The next day, Thursday, the first of February, I called my church and asked to be put on the prayer chain. Although I was in shock, I was very hopeful. It couldn't be as bad as it appeared. Denial had also set in. That night I sent my second e-mail to my friends:

It is 9:15 and I have finally completed all the phone calls to my kids.... We saw Dr. G. in Bellingham this afternoon, taking the CT scan X-rays with us. He was a wonderful man who spent over an hour with us, going over the X-rays in detail explaining all the different kinds of brain tumors and what is involved with each of them. The tumor is quite large, is on the right side with a smaller one growing on the left side..... While the tumors on both sides can be reached surgically and probably would not be too difficult to remove, there is a connecting growth between the 2 halves of the brain. This part would be both difficult and risky to remove. While he couldn't say for sure whether it was benign or malignant, it looked to him like it was a Glioblastnoma or Stage IV malignant tumor.

I am holding up pretty well right now. Sometimes it really hits me and I weep. But when I talk about it, there seems to be hope – at least for the moment. I am praying that God will direct us to the right surgeon. I feel that God has given us some time and that He won't take him away from me right now – that we will still have some time together. The family is so concerned.

I am feeling the support of your prayers, and I am soliciting as many prayers from others as I can. I have been reading in Luke and the Psalms and God keeps giving me words of faith and hope to cling to. I know He will be with us. Thank you so much. I feel your hugs and prayers through the Internet – I really do.

I was in shock. The brain registered the news, but it wouldn't - couldn't - grasp the totality of the fact that Le Roy was going to die. I clung to hope as though it were a lifeline that would pull me out of the water I was drowning in. To contemplate the thought that Le Roy might actually die was too much. I couldn't process it. I don't think Le Roy did or could either. Hope kept me alive. Later it would become a two-edged sword.

Friday was a blur: concern for Le Roy; hiccups that started the night before and kept getting worse; calls from our doctors about getting neurosurgeon appointments in Seattle; a trip to Emergency to get help for the hiccups. The only medication they could give him that would give any relief for such severe hiccups was Thorazine, an anti-psychotic drug that worked on the nervous system that triggers the hiccups. I was so grateful they had something that would stop them. However, I would soon come to hate it as well. With the addition of all these drugs and the aggressive advance of the tumor, it seemed Le Roy was starting down a slippery slope.

However, when I re-read my journal entry for that morning at a later time, my writing still conveyed hope and peace.

My Journal:
MRI scheduled for 7:30 tomorrow morning in Bellingham. More calls. We are being referred to a more prominent brain surgeon in Seattle, and got some medication to help curb the terrible hiccups that racked Le Roy's body all through the night, shaking both of us awake many times with such an intensity that even the bed seemed to shake.

And we had a visit from Pastor Kevin - a wonderful visit - time spent in sharing events of our lives and a wonderful prayer. Part of that prayer was that God would give us a sign each day of hope and peace – that He is in this with us. How fortunate we are to have such a caring and compassionate pastor. Then there was a visit from Barbara and Skip and a call from Ruth, my dear sister-in-law, in Sioux Falls. And another call from Ron in Los Angeles, "I will do anything you need of me. I will get on a plane and be there in a few hours. I will take out the garbage. Anything you need, just ask." [Ron was one of Le Roy's former students who now lived and composed music in Los Angeles].

And the e-mail responses from all over of people praying and holding us up to God for miracles and healing. We are being supported, surrounded, cushioned, and insulated by all these prayers. They are lifting up our spirits, and giving us a peace and calm that would be impossible to generate on our own - an amazing phenomenon - impossible to put into words. Scripture says we shall have "peace that passes all understanding" and it's true. How can anyone go through the harshness and crises of life without having a faith, or without experiencing God's love, mercy and Grace?

Saturday. It was now less than a week since Le Roy was diagnosed. From Wednesday until this morning the medications and rapid advance of the tumor had already changed him from a functioning person to one so blunted, so deadened to affect, that he literally seemed like a walking zombie. Le Roy had always been a morning person, but now I could hardly wake him. In the past, he rarely, if ever, took medications - even for headaches. Now his system was being bombarded and overloaded with them. And the physical and mental result was both dramatic and shocking. He no longer was Le Roy.

Our friends, Skip and Barbara, insisted on taking us to the hospital in Bellingham that morning. Since the hospital was trying to accommodate us within their full schedule we had to be at the hospital ready to take the MRI by eight in the morning. It was a forty-five minute drive and in the car Le Roy's hiccups began again. I knew he had to have that MRI before he could see more brain tumor specialists and I knew he couldn't take it if he couldn't lie perfectly still. So at the hospital I gave him the maximum dosage of Thorazine. The hiccups stopped, but afterward Skip and I had to help him stand upright as his legs kept buckling. I don't know which I hated more: the hiccups or the Thorazine.

Saturday was developing into a beautiful and sunny day, so after we returned home I decided to drive to Seattle with Le Roy to visit our daughter Elizabeth, Gene and our new granddaughter, Aria. In the midst of this trauma, I still remained optimistic and hopeful. On our way, we stopped by Denny and Joanne's house, friends of ours who lived near by. Joanne told us she had awakened at four in the morning and was filled with an incredible peace about Le Roy. It was so overwhelming that she could only lie there and praise God for His goodness and knew that God was with us. And that was how I had felt early that morning, as my journal reflected:

My Journal:
When I awoke at six and gave Le Roy his pill and spent time reading my Bible, I could only thank and praise Him for the love and care and prayers of everyone who were supporting us. It is truly remarkable. I feel not only surrounded but encapsulated in a cocoon, floating on and through the harsh realities swirling around us.

Again, words could not describe this amazing phenomenon, and it was one I experienced many times during those early days of our journey. It was like living in a twilight zone. I was there experiencing all the trauma and day to day crises, and felt the deep fear and anxiety. And yet, it seemed as if I were going through this on one level while also moving through it on another; as though I were looking down upon myself making the decisions and choices that would hopefully bring the treatment to my husband which he needed – right now - to save his life.

I know that even though I was experiencing deep denial, I was also being given deep peace and hope. Are these "straws" we grab hold of mental crutches needed to survive? Or are they real supports given to us by God in order to survive? It seemed every time I opened my Bible, God's finger would point to a page and scripture I needed. Without even realizing it, I was turning every day to the Psalms and each day a Psalm would lift me up and give me incredible strength and even joy. This was God's way of helping me survive. It was God's blessing for me.

I underlined those Psalms and wrote beside them in the margins of my Bible substituting words such as "enemy" with "cancer," and putting Le Roy's and my names in places where it was appropriate to what we were experiencing. Some verses struck me so forcefully, that I copied them into my journal. This was the one for today:

Psalm 16:1-2; 7-11
"*Preserve me, O God, for in thee I take refuge. I say to the Lord, 'Thou Art my Lord. I have no good apart from Thee.' I bless the Lord who gives me counsel; in the night also my heart instructs me. I keep the Lord always before me; because he is at my right hand, I shall not be moved. Therefore, my heart is glad, and my soul rejoices; my body also dwells secure. For thou dost not give me up to Sheol, or let the godly one see the Pit. Thou dost show me the path of life; in thy presence there is fulness of joy, in thy right hand are pleasures for evermore.*"

A week had gone by. It seemed like an eternity. But it was only the beginning.

Chapter 3

From Crisis to Crisis

*I*t is said that your life flashes through your mind in a few seconds when you are drowning. It seemed that we had already lived a whole lifetime during this past week. And while yesterday had been a promise of spring, today was a reminder that we were still in winter. The weather along with our lives had dramatically changed.

My Journal:
The skies are leaden. A steady rain falls. My spirits are down as well. My body is tired. I forced myself to stay awake until midnight to give Le Roy his pill. We fudged fifteen minutes. I woke at 6:30 to discover Le Roy's body racked with terrible hiccups. After giving him a Decadron, we were able to sleep for another hour, but whenever he moved the hiccups would start again. I will be carried by the prayers of others today. I am getting so tired. Mustn't get sick.

   "Hear a just cause, O Lord; attend to my cry! Give ear to my prayer from lips free of deceit. I call upon thee, for thou wilt answer me, O God; incline thy ear to me, hear my words. Arise O Lord! confront them, overthrow them! [the tumor cells, Oh God]." (Psalm 17:1; 6; 13)

   The Le Roy I knew was disappearing before my eyes. He had such an amazing mind. He not only was an accomplished musician and band leader, but he designed our home, built a music department from scratch, and developed the musical talents of students who attended the college where he taught or took private music lessons from him. Le Roy had the amazing ability to wrap his mind around a problem and arrive at a logical and working outcome in a short amount of time. And now, that was all slipping away and he was functioning by the disciplined habits of the past.

This would be my last journal entry for a long time because there wouldn't be any time to write. But I kept a progress log, and continued sending e-mail updates and prayer requests to friends and family because we desperately needed their prayers. And they desperately wanted to hear some good news from me.

If the prior week had been a blur, then this week was becoming a nightmare. When Le Roy's doctor tried to schedule a neurosurgeon's appointment for him with his HMO, he was told they couldn't see him until March 17th. Without treatment, Le Roy would have been dead by then. But a consultation appointment was made for Wednesday with a prominent neurosurgeon in Seattle who was outside of our health care provider.

Late Monday afternoon, our HMO's receptionist called to inform us that we had an appointment scheduled with one of their neurosurgeons in Seattle the next morning at 11:30. When I expressed my surprise and hesitancy, since I understood no appointment was possible until March, she told me that if I wanted to be treated by them I had better take the appointment. So did I want it or not! Her attitude and words were like a pail of ice water thrown over me, adding to the already high level of shock and trauma I was experiencing. I said we would be there.

Denny and Joanne, our friends who had been praying and keeping in touch daily, insisted on driving us Tuesday morning. Seattle was an hour and a half away. Elizabeth and Gene, who lived in Seattle, would meet us there with our beautiful infant granddaughter. How glad I was to have friends who were so eager to help. We needed their hands on the wheel and to be there to hold us and cry and pray with us after we saw the doctor.

The neurosurgeon's words were like the tolling of a death knoll. He gave us little hope for any time remaining for Le Roy. In fact he talked to us as though Le Roy weren't even there. After answering a few questions, Le Roy never responded to what the doctor was saying in any way. I wondered how much of what he heard was actually being processed and retained. I had always tried to respect Le Roy's quiet reactions to events. He never liked to talk about negative things, because as he might say, what is there to talk about. He would process them, figure out solutions if that was what was needed, and move on. It was a long ride home.

Wednesday morning I sent the following e-mail to my friends. It had been one week since Le Roy had the CT scan that revealed his tumor.

Dearest friends,
God has blessed us yet again. I want you to know that we were able to sleep all night with no hiccups at all. When I woke at six to give Le Roy his pill, he was sleeping peacefully and afterwards I was able to go back to sleep for another hour. That is truly remarkable, because I only gave him a regular dosage of Thorazine last night.

His sleeping late in the morning has given me an opportunity to read my Bible and pray. And the psalm the Lord had for me this morning was Psalm 18 and it seemed it was written for me. God not only is my rock and strength, but He has reached down from on high and draws us both out of the muddy waters of anxiety, uncertainties, and negative diagnosis....

I had a long talk with Frank [he and his wife were friends of ours] this morning and conveyed my words of praise to him as well and he told me about his vision in church with hands surrounding Le Roy's head. When I close my eyes and talk to God, I see all these bundles and bundles of prayers at God's feet, and I am immediately reminded of Luke 11:5-13.
I love you all and your prayers are sustaining me.
Love, Marlene

I saved these e-mails because they had become my journals. These were friends who lived in Shelter Bay and wintered in Arizona. I am amazed at how much peace and hope God was giving me in the midst of all this. I am amazed I was able to see all the blessings that

God was sending me as well. God was touching the lives and hearts of my friends as well and they shared God's blessings and hope with me in return. How amazing is that. I guess at times like this you realize just how much we are the family of God.

On Wednesday we returned to Seattle for our consultation appointment with Dr. N. This time I felt comfortable driving. Again Elizabeth and Gene were there with Aria. They also were exhausted as every three hours Elizabeth had to nurse and care for Aria who had been born a few days short of being considered premature.

What a different neurosurgeon this man was. What a wonderful comfort he was to us. While he did not extend false hope, neither did he take hope away from us. His exam was more complete and gentler in delivery. When he asked questions of Le Roy they were soft spoken and his answers revealed how much Le Roy lacked in awareness. Le Roy said we were in the wrong month, didn't know what day it was or what year it was. He couldn't remember what happened a month ago. The prognosis from both neurosurgeons was the same: inoperable; needed a biopsy as quickly as possible so treatment could begin; and all indicators pointed to a Level IV, very aggressive Glioblastnoma brain tumor.

But while the other doctor gave him weeks to live, this man softened the blow by indicating that the time Le Roy had left was hard to predict and gave examples of patients who he believed wouldn't live through the week but who had surprised him by living for two years. So while we were beginning to accept the fact that Le Roy's time was limited, we still left feeling encouraged and hopeful that we had some time and whatever time that was it would be enough.

Our youngest son, Don, had flown in that afternoon from Los Angeles and we all gathered at our daughter's house for dinner to discuss the options before us. We knew that Le Roy had to have a biopsy before he could get treatment and that he needed treatment immediately. We all wanted Dr. N. to do the biopsy even if that meant paying for it ourselves as I was prepared to pay whatever it would have cost; but he was unavailable until the following week. The HMO neurosurgeon was prepared to get him into the hospital the next day and do the biopsy on Friday. We all agreed to go ahead with the HMO doctor. Le Roy seemed oblivious to our conversation.

Our other son, Bob, who lived in Portland, Oregon, arrived late Wednesday night. Early Thursday morning we started calling our HMO in Seattle to schedule the biopsy. To our dismay and alarm all we got was the cancer clinic's answering machine! The HMO's operator couldn't help us either. It seemed there was nobody in the neurological cancer clinic that could take our calls, and we were instructed to wait until the surgical nurse returned from morning surgery to schedule us, and nobody seemed to know when that was going to be. We began to panic, especially when Le Roy got sick and threw up in bed. He had eaten compulsively the night before and we had difficulty getting him to stop. Now his stomach was rebelling. He didn't even seem to be aware that he had thrown up.

With a hurried and frantic call to our primary care physician we were sent to emergency again. By this time it was almost noon. Our pastor was scheduled to arrive around one o'clock, and friends were bringing dinner, but we still hadn't reached the neurosurgeon to schedule Le Roy's biopsy. He was getting sicker by the minute. I didn't have time to clean up the bed before leaving with our two boys, their cell phones in hand, to drive to the ER. It wasn't until late that afternoon that the ER doctors were finally able to reach the neurosurgeon who told us to bring Le Roy to Seattle immediately and check him into the hospital. If he were already checked in the hospital would be pressured to schedule his biopsy the next day.

It was 5:30 in the afternoon when we arrived home from the ER to prepare to drive to Seattle. Denny and Joanne had just arrived with our dinner. There was no time to eat – in fact nobody was hungry. Our oldest son had already left to drive the four hours back to Portland to return the next day with his family. The food was put in the refrigerator, I assured them I could drive to Seattle, and asked them to take care of our little dog for us. Don, Le Roy and I were on the road in a half hour.

Since the gas tank was registering empty we stopped for gas before getting on the freeway. And then another crisis occurred. Le Roy kept trying to get out of the car to put the gas in the car. He was unable to process our pleas to stay in the car and it really shook us up. He kept playing with the button that opened his window and our son in the back seat was afraid that he might open the door while we were driving. (Thank God for driver controls over door and window locks.) He was no longer our Le Roy. It was really hard on our son to see his bright, articulate, intelligent and responsible dad reacting as an impulsive child. It was one of the longest drives I have ever made.

We didn't see the neurosurgeon until late the following afternoon. By this time our oldest son had returned with his family and the doctor met with all the members of our family before the surgery. His words were chilling: "...it probably would be better for everyone if he died on the operating table." I couldn't believe a physician would say that to a family at this time. I felt a cold, horrible chill and dread in my heart that Le Roy might die at the hands of this calloused surgeon! If the biopsy had not been necessary in order to get treatment, I would have stopped it.

Around five in the afternoon, they took him into surgery and the family gathered in the hallway outside the operating room to wait and pray. I finally broke down and started crying and it was my youngest son who gently took my hand and prayed for us. What a comforting prayer. As I sat there waiting, I remember thinking, please God don't let him die on the operating table. And the image of a child asking his parent for just one more cookie entered my mind, and the parent, out of love, obliged. "Please God, just one more cookie – just a little more time – don't take him like this! Please Lord!" And God gave us that extra time to absorb and prepare for his impending death.

The biopsy relieved enough pressure on the brain, so that when they wheeled him out of surgery, his delightful wit and humor returned for a short while and we saw a little bit of the "old Le Roy" again. Humor came so easily to him. To see the humorous side of anything was as natural as breathing to him.

We had to stay another night in the hospital. I not only was allowed to stay with him in his room, but was also told I could sleep in the hospital bed with him if I wanted. I was so grateful, and although it was very cramped, it somehow "normalized" what was happening. I was able to lie with my head on his shoulder with his arms wrapped around me. I also knew that he would not be able to get out of bed and injure himself as long as I was there beside him.

I remembered how difficult it had been to keep him in the car when we stopped for gas.

The hospital pathology lab results were inconclusive. The biopsy sample wasn't good. However, the biopsy was sent to an outside lab, but we had to wait until Monday or Tuesday of the following week to see whether their more extensive testing could give us a definitive answer. We were warned that without a conclusive result, treatment couldn't begin. Even so, the ride home Saturday afternoon was easier than the trip to the hospital. I felt the other lab would soon give us the information we needed to begin treatment.

It was a long weekend. Le Roy kept getting up in the middle of the night to go to the bathroom and then would forget to come back to bed. He would start going through bathroom drawers, sorting and cleaning them or just fiddling with the contents. I feared he might take some medication he found. I slept with one eye open and was becoming more hyper-alert and vigilant to any movement he made in bed so that I would wake up whenever he did. Even during the day, we had to be alert to whatever he might do. Although he seemed tired and rested a lot, he suddenly would get up and start going through the kitchen drawers. Once he took out a large kitchen knife and tried to cut a piece of paper with it. Another time he took out a meat cleaver and tried to open some mail. I was afraid to leave him alone unattended for any length of time. The tumor was eating away at his brain more and more leaving me this man who appeared to be in the last stages of Alzheimer's.

In the midst of all this, the telephone kept ringing from friends in shock and dismay asking, "What can I do?" Our sons were extremely concerned because I too was changing before their eyes. I was getting very exhausted and they knew it would be impossible for me to be awake and watchful 24 hours a day. But who could help me? Who could stay with me? As an artist who contracted out his services, it was imperative that my son Don return to Santa Monica to be available for work. Bob had a family, was working and going to college at night. Elizabeth and Gene were exhausted from lack of sleep because of little Aria's nursing schedule. Already our friends were working overtime to help in any way they could. What should I do?

The only person I could think who might be able to help us was our long time dear friend Dede who lived with her husband Tom in England where he worked. With an anxious and fearful heart I called her. Without hesitation she said, "I'll be there as soon as I can get a flight."

On Sunday, I updated friends and family with the following e-mail:

I know I have taken awhile to get this information off to you, but it has been so hectic - there hasn't been a moment to do one more thing. It seems years have gone by already, condensed into one short week and a half. I want to thank everyone who has been praying for us. I close my eyes and see all the prayers heaped at God's feet. I can feel your prayers and God's loving arms sustaining me, floating us along.

The news is not good. We have seen three neurosurgeons. They all concur as to the prognosis. It looks like the tumor is a Glioblastnoma – a fast growing malignant tumor that has invaded both sides of Le Roy's brain. It is inoperable – there is too much mass and it would amount to a lobotomy...

Le Roy knows he has a tumor but the pressure on the brain determines how much he is with us mentally at any time. Usually in the morning he is brighter, but by night time he is like a person in the later stages of Alzheimer's although he still recognizes all of us. He is on a lot of medications to reduce the swelling and to prevent seizures...

Thank you for your prayers and please keep praying. You have no idea how powerful your prayers are and how much they are supporting us. And please pray for my three kids as well. It is so hard on them. Little Aria is doing well and growing every day and is a ray of God's sunshine in all of this.
Love to all of you,
Marlene and Le Roy

Friends. How can I begin to put into words what they have meant to us? They were there – immediately – without being asked. Those who were wintering in Arizona sent e-mails filled with encouragement, prayers, praises and promises of God's love for us. When they said they were praying many times a day, they meant it. Those who were here were driving us, praying with us, bringing us meals, and taking care of our little dog, often at a moment's notice and for as long as was necessary. One couple had just returned home from Arizona for a couple of weeks when Le Roy went to the hospital for his biopsy. They called and asked what they could do. I didn't know what to tell them. Without a moment's hesitation they went to our home and cleaned our entire house. They changed the sheets that still had the vomit on them, washed them, dried the mattress and remade the bed; cleaned the toilets and vacuumed and washed floors. We returned from the hospital in Seattle to find a clean and sparkling home. I was overwhelmed with such a gift of love! Thank you, May and Frank! But they didn't stop there. Every day they came over and sometimes stayed the night. They took us to our first meeting with the oncologist and then to Le Roy's first radiation treatment. By Monday we were in a holding pattern, anxiously waiting for the results of the biopsy. Le Roy's primary doctor had scheduled an appointment for Thursday with an oncologist at a local cancer clinic. Tuesday morning a neurosurgeon from our HMO called to inform us that the pathology report could not conclusively say whether Le Roy's tumor was a Glioblastnoma, and that we would have to schedule another biopsy right away. And if that didn't produce a good sample then they would actually have to do surgery, removing a larger piece of the tumor (and brain).

    I felt like somebody had rammed me with a ten-ton truck! How could they even suggest doing brain surgery when all the neurosurgeons had agreed it was out of the question! And there wasn't time to do another biopsy! Le Roy needed treatment now! With my eldest son and our pastor listening I argued my case with this doctor who informed me that Le Roy couldn't get treatment without an accurate pathology report and warned us that if we proceeded with treatment without it, we could actually harm him!

    I hung up stunned. My son and pastor suggested I call the neurosurgeon we had consulted and who we all liked so well. We weren't even his patients, but he took my phone call and gently answered my questions. While he was prepared to do another biopsy on Le Roy, he said he believed they could start treatment without it. He also gave us his stamp of approval on the cancer clinic and oncologist I would be seeing!

I immediately phoned the oncologist we were scheduled to meet on Thursday and relayed my concerns and the neurosurgeon's words. He listened and quietly said he not only would treat Le Roy without a more conclusive pathology report, but the treatment would be the same whether it was a Glioblastnoma or not.

Thank you God! I let out my breath and breathed again.

Two weeks had gone by.

Chapter 4

Denial

Le Roy's treatment began Thursday, February 15th. While the prognosis wasn't good, we still maintained our hope that we had some quality time left – a hope that would rise and fall like the tides over time. Since that fateful day in January, we had simply been in survival mode, but now that treatment had started we felt that Le Roy might be able to beat the odds and live for a while.

Two couples, long time friends, helped me take Le Roy to this first meeting with the oncologist as he was still very unpredictable (opening a door while the car was in motion was a major concern), and the medications made him very drowsy. In fact, Le Roy was unable to stay awake through that first meeting with the oncologist, a kind and compassionate man who took the time to explain the treatment program including how they would shape a face mask that would hold Le Roy's head firmly in place during treatments. This was done by placing a wet, flexible webbing over the face which quickly hardened into a stiff meshed mask, the sides of which could be fastened to the X-ray table.

There would be a total of thirty-five treatments, one each day for six weeks, five days a week. The first twenty-five treatments would focus on the large tumor in the frontal lobes plus one or two centimeters around the mass and then the last ten treatments would spot focus on any remaining, growing tumor areas, going deep inside his brain to reach the cells that had wrapped themselves around the corpus callosum. A CT scan would then be taken to assess what progress had been made.

The next day I received this e-mail from a friend in Arizona:

From Lamentations 3:22-23
"The steadfast love of the Lord never ceases, his mercies never come to an end; they are new every morning; great is thy faithfulness." May this reality be new and alive in your life each day as you walk through the Valley of the Shadow. Lynn

I didn't feel as though I was going through the valley of the shadow of death as yet, but later on I would recall her e-mail and re-read it. But for now, I was soaking up all the overwhelming love and support and prayers of my friends, and hung onto the hope that Le Roy would survive. I returned her e-mail:

Your thoughts, prayers and poems have been so uplifting. I can't even tell you. They get printed out so I can read them over and over again. I am sending an update in a little while, but it seems the whole picture is changing. We are delighted with the radial oncologist and Le Roy has had two treatments. Already we can see a difference! It's as though God has opened a door and nothing can touch us now. There are five percent of people who live beyond two years after radiation. I don't know whether Le Roy is in that five percent or not, but it no longer makes a difference. Whatever time he has left will be enough and will be crammed with all the love we can muster. I am praying each day that God will bless a hundredfold all of you who have been holding us in prayer. God bless you both. Love, Marlene

That first weekend after treatment started we were inundated with friends and family who came to visit, and by the time most of them had gone home Saturday night Le Roy was exhausted. As he sat in the recliner watching TV he suddenly got up and said he felt funny. He came to sit beside me at the kitchen counter and tried to tell me what was happening. He felt a tightening in his chest and his stomach was a little upset. While he sat telling me this he had another episode. He was having difficulty explaining what was happening. I rubbed his neck and shoulders and back thinking that all the company had tired him so much and maybe this would help him relax.

While I was rubbing, he had what we now believe was another little seizure occurring on his right side. It was like a "rolling" up his muscles from the waist to the neck. I called the doctor's office and was told to take Le Roy to emergency as quickly as possible. The doctor and I both believed he was in the early stages of having a major seizure. The hospital ER did not have an EEG to measure brain wave activity, but a blood test revealed his anti-seizure medication was too low and they increased the level of Dilantin and Thorazine. It was almost two in the morning before we finally got home. The doctors told me it now was very important to have his head elevated when he was lying down. The next day Frank purchased a foam wedge for Le Roy to use so we wouldn't have to get a hospital bed - yet.

Dede arrived from England on the eighteenth of February; three days after treatment had begun. Before she arrived, teams of rotating friends came over to the house almost every day, either sitting with Le Roy while I ran errands, or bringing meals and staying to eat with us. Sometimes they stayed the night. It took almost a week of treatment before Le Roy stopped getting up at night. And during that time, I had to remain super vigilant. There was little time to complete all the preventions necessary to keep him safe.

One night when he got up in the middle of the night, he locked the bathroom door and I couldn't get him to open it. After a frantic search, I finally found a key and opened the door just in time to see him prying open a prescription bottle of medicine I didn't know was there. I was able to coax him back to bed, but it was a long time before I could go back to sleep. By the time Dede arrived I was exhausted - physically, mentally and emotionally.

It was so good to have Dede here! Le Roy and Dede had been such good friends and they had always fed off each other's humor. We had claimed her as "sister" as both she and Le Roy had been an only child. Both her parents and Le Roy's were deceased. She became our security blanket and gradually I was able to relax. I had someone there full time to help observe and share Le Roy's progress. The steps were very small, but to us they seemed monumental!

Le Roy had been the most intelligent and logical man I had ever known. He had a wonderful ability to think through problems before acting upon possible solutions. He loved to solve problems, whatever they were, whether he was working with students, running a music department, arranging music, designing a house and building it or simply taking care of daily mechanical and household problems as they occurred. He was quiet and methodical in his problem solving and thinking. So every step we saw him take towards this same person we knew was like the sweetest sunshine.

We settled into a semi-stable existence as we made a truce with the cancer and the radiation began its job. As Le Roy reclaimed some of his mental ability, I was able to relax even more and became less vigilant, although he still exhibited some compulsive behavior. But as time went on, that behavior became less threatening to his personal safety.

We were being lulled into a false reality by this initial positive response to treatment. My denial system kicked into full gear. He was going to make it! We would have at least a couple of years! He would fight this and beat it! I started to chronicle a daily progress report that would continue until his death four weeks after treatment ended.

Chapter 5

A Reprieve

As the treatments began to reduce the swelling and tissue mass, I was determined to help Le Roy restore his thinking capacity and constantly tried to think of ways to accomplish that goal. I gave him the mail to open, and he would fill out the marketing cards found in magazines. I bought simple mind-game puzzles and crossword puzzle books. I would give him one and would ask him to help me with mine. I considered every word he used and every word he gave me as proof that he was getting well.

He was always good at cards, so I started playing solitaire with him. At first he could only place the cards in rows or line them up in some kind of order. Order seemed to be very important to him. But gradually, over several weeks, Le Roy was actually able to play a game of solitaire with only a minimal amount of help from me.

February 21st - E-mail update to friends and family
This week I can send good news! Le Roy has now had six treatments and they have done wonders! He is joking and carrying on a conversation again. He still has trouble remembering and has difficulty with short-term memory and processing information. But the progress he has made is truly remarkable considering how bad he was and we are very encouraged!

This is Dede's second week with us and we are so thankful that she flew home from England to spend this time helping us. It really makes a difference having someone else here all the time. People phone and say they are bringing us dinner or call and ask if they can run any errands. One of our many friends has organized a car pool to take Le Roy to all six weeks of his radiation treatments. Where else could you live and have such a wonderful sense of community, love, support and caring as we do here in Shelter Bay?

The radiation treatments make him sleepy and he naps a lot of the time. But today, he has been up almost all day. And he is sleeping through the nights and the terrible hiccups have not returned...

Thank you for your prayers. They are being answered as God is blessing us every day.

It was amazing that God was able to help me see all those little blessings. We were on a journey that neither of us wanted to be on, but God never left us. He was always there at our side. We were encouraged to believe that what was happening in the moment would extend into the future as well. We continued to believe that maybe we would beat the odds and he would make a complete recovery. Denial is a remarkable survival system. Without the hope for a positive future, we wouldn't have enjoyed and been able to share our love for each other during those last days as our focus would have been on death, grief and loss instead.

One day when I returned from grocery shopping, Dede met me in the garage. She was ecstatic! While I was gone, Le Roy decided to drill a hole in a flattened penny to insert a chain for one of the grand kids. It was such a simple little thing. But because the tumor had taken away his ability to evaluate his actions, it had become a big thing. Dede was quite concerned about letting him work with his tools for fear he might hurt himself. But both of us tried to continue to treat him with respect in the face of this disease. So she asked if she could watch while he worked and was elated when he handled the drill press and tools with his old level of expertise. Didn't this mean he was getting better? We measured success by the teaspoonful and felt they were giant strides forward.

Another sign of just how far he had improved occurred one day after a trip to the doctor. He was having an especially good day, and we decided to stop and have lunch at a nearby restaurant. A week earlier this would not have been possible. He held the restaurant door open for us, joked with the waitress and with us, and carried on a regular conversation. He ordered his own lunch, and with only a little help was able to tally the bill and pay for the food. Simple, everyday events that we all take for granted. But I was elated! I felt we had just climbed Mt. Everest! Wasn't this more proof of his progress? Didn't this mean he was recovering and would get well?

The treatments were permitting him to process information and retrieve and connect it with what was in his memory. After nine treatments, Le Roy's ability to remain alert enabled him to discuss business and financial issues. He went with me to see our attorney to make important corrections to our Living Trust and then to our bank to have our signatures notarized. It truly was a milestone.

Prior to the diagnosis, Le Roy and I had planned to sell our house and design a smaller house to build. Buoyed by Le Roy's remarkable comeback, I put our house up for sale. It helped me believe we still had a future together. By the end of February the oncologist was very encouraged at Le Roy's progress and indicated to us that this early progress was a good sign for long-term recovery. Somehow, I felt we had beaten the odds. I was sure we would have at least a couple of years together!

I sent this encouraging e-mail to all our friends and family on Monday, March 5th:

Le Roy has now had 11 treatments out of the 36 he will receive over the course of 5-6 weeks. Are we back to normal yet? No. I'm sure the tumor hasn't disappeared. And I know we have a long road ahead of us. But the improvements have been exciting, very noticeable and very encouraging. His tumor had taken him down so rapidly during those first two weeks that he literally seemed at death's door. When he started treatments, I had to help him get out of bed, help him shave, sponge bathe him, help him get dressed and put on his shoes and stockings. Anything he could do for himself required constant supervision for him to be able to follow through.

I still have to wake him and get him started on his morning routines, but he is now able to shave and brush his teeth, shower and dress himself. Because he still doesn't have a sense of time urgency and needs to leave the house by 10:15 for his 11:00 treatment, I lay out his clothes and remind him to hurry. However, I am no longer afraid to leave him alone for short periods of time.

While he still can't retrieve all of his long-term memory and his short-term memory is still affected, we are seeing improvements every day. He will say to people, "They tell me I have been sick and have a tumor," but he has no recollection of it. But last night he told a friend over the phone about his radiation treatments and what happens during treatment. I know enough about the procedure to verify that it was a correct memory.

I started playing solitaire with him a week ago. When we first started playing, he could shuffle the deck, but he needed help laying down the cards correctly and playing the deck in his hand. He could match cards on his own, but wanted to play all the cards at once. Last Friday, he played the game correctly himself with only a few reminders here and there!

He has gone from responding with short remarks to people to initiating conversation. His sense of humor has returned and he jokes about things that are happening. He was able to talk about our house and things we did when we were building. At times he seems completely like his old self. At other times, however, because of the radiation he is still very tired. While this might not sound like much, to those of us who saw him so sick, it is truly miraculous and we are very encouraged. We continue to ask God for complete healing. As I talk to people, they share stories of other people who were told they had six months to live and are still living after 5-10-20 years.

So I ask for your continued prayers that Le Roy will be completely healed, if it is God's will. I know miracles happen – He gives me little miracles and blessings every day! Right now I am just content knowing that He is at work in our lives, and I know that whatever time we have left will be enough time. I am continually upheld by the prayers that are being said for us and I pray each day that God will bless each of you who are so faithfully praying for us. Thank you everyone – for your time and love and help!
Love, Marlene

And life settled into a comfortable routine. Although I could now leave him alone for short periods of time, these early days were not always a smooth uphill progress. One day he might do exceedingly well but the next he would slide back a little, be more tired, and I would have to remind him to finish things. And yet, after two weeks of treatments, he had made enormous progress towards recovery. One day as I was telling our pastor that I was planning to bring Le Roy to church with me, he said he would be so elated he would cry a river. He would consider it a miracle as he knew how sick Le Roy had been. I told him I would bring him a box of Kleenex. Le Roy went to church with me that Sunday and the smiles were greater than the tears and the Kleenex was not needed.

After a few weeks we felt Le Roy had recovered enough for Dede to return home. We were both confident that when she and Tom returned in the summer, we would be back doing things together as usual. We couldn't have imagined that when they returned, he would be dead.

It was so hard to say goodbye to Dede that rainy mid-March day and both Le Roy and I had tears in our eyes when she left. We had come to depend upon her being there and I was struck with an overwhelming sense of loss and being totally alone. After those first few frantic weeks, our friends had resumed their lives as well. One couple returned to Arizona. Another couple left to go on a missionary trip. Although Le Roy was getting better, I knew I still couldn't leave him alone for a long period of time and since the radiation left him quite tired, it was hard to take him with me when I had to run errands. And an ominous pall of gloom settled over me as I tried to remain focused on the three good weeks we just had.

Chapter 6

Fear Returns

But things quickly began to happen that made that pall of gloom become a reality. The three weeks with Dede had lulled all of us into a false sense of hope, believing he really was going to recover.

The first sign that things weren't as good as we thought came shortly after Dede left for England. Saturday, March seventeenth, the day before my birthday, I noticed that Le Roy had developed a cough and seemed to be getting short of breath. However, it wasn't so bad that I felt he was actually getting sick. So, I followed through with our plans to drive to Seattle for a birthday lunch my daughter had prepared for me. I knew she wanted to see her dad too. In the hour and a half it took for us to get to Seattle, Le Roy's color had become pasty and as soon as we finished eating, we headed back home. By the time we arrived home Le Roy's breathing was labored and I had difficulty getting him from the car into the house. I was panicking. A call to the doctor sent me scurrying to the hospital - again - with the possibility that Le Roy might have pneumonia.

The emergency room is not one of my favorite places even though it is a lifeline when a crisis occurs. That day, it was full of families with sick children and I was even more alarmed that he would catch something that would take his life. Our friends, Denny and Joanne, who had just returned from their missionary trip, called and immediately drove to the hospital to sit with us as we waited our turn to see the doctor.

Finally, after over an hour, Le Roy was taken to one of the cubicles to see a doctor. His blood was drawn and sent to the lab, and he was sent for X-rays. His oxygen levels were very low, and they put an oxygen mask on him. Le Roy hated it and constantly tried to take it off. Any mental processing ability he had gained was now receding rapidly. While we waited for the results of the blood test, I struggled to keep the oxygen mask on him. Just before midnight the ER doctors decided that he had a viral pneumonia and they were going to admit him to the hospital. This was very serious as it is very difficult to treat a viral pneumonia.

I had always been allowed to stay with family members when they were admitted to the hospital, often times spending the night when it was appropriate. I told the medical staff that I would go home, take care of my dog, change into some comfortable clothes and be back to spend the night with Le Roy. But when I returned, I discovered much to my dismay, that they were putting him in a room with another elderly gentleman as there wasn't a private room available. Hospital policy didn't allow wives to stay in the room when another man was present. And even though this person was asleep, hard of hearing, and the curtain was drawn between the beds, the nurses and staff were quite adamant that I leave. I was feeling panicked again because Le Roy was still constantly trying to remove his oxygen mask. Finally I realized I had no choice but to leave, but not before I made the staff promise to post an aide outside his door for the night to keep his oxygen mask on.

When I returned the next morning, Le Roy's doctor had already been in to see him and had read the riot act to the hospital. They found a private room that morning and I not only was allowed to stay the night, but was encouraged by both his doctor and the hospital staff to sleep in the extra bed in the room.

What a wonderful primary physician my husband had! I don't know how we would have made it through this terrible journey without his careful, methodical investigations into what was happening to Le Roy. He was not convinced that he had viral pneumonia and ordered a CT scan which revealed blood clots lodged in his lungs.

With Thankful Hearts

Psalm 18
143

After a quick consultation with the oncologist about the risk of potential bleeding in the brain, they both felt that Le Roy was far enough along with his treatments that the risk would be minimal if he stopped radiation and was given blood thinners to dissolve the clots. Le Roy was started on anti-coagulant shots and Coumadin.

The following night, I sat in a recliner beside Le Roy's bed hoping that I would be able to keep an eye on him and still get some cat naps. Hah! It was a terrible night! With more oxygen to the brain, Le Roy was more cognizant of his oxygen mask. I had to be awake and stay alert the whole night in order to keep it on him. At times I literally had to fight with him as he became more belligerent ("I have decided I do not need this any more. It is making my chest sore!") This was so out of character for him. But in another way it was not, because he always trusted his judgment. So actually, it was a positive sign that he was getting better. But it didn't make my job any easier, and around three in the morning he declared that he wasn't going to wear it anymore - period!

Desperate, I called the nurse, who tried to placate him. Wrong thing to do! He said to her, "I have been a college teacher for thirty years and I know what I need and I don't need this." In her most condescending voice, she tried to humor him, and asked what he taught and with a matched sarcasm he replied, "I taught music." But when she asked what musical instrument he played, I saw the wheels churning in a brain that was recovering. In less than a second he replied, "An ophicleide!"

I laughed out loud! Puzzled, she looked at me to see whether there was such an instrument. I told her there was, but I had no intention of telling her anything more about it. I wasn't going to spoil this moment for Le Roy. If she wanted to know what it was, she was going to have to ask him. I knew he was very aware of what he said, because an ophicleide is the name for an ancient wind instrument consisting of a long, tapering brass tube bent double with keys - a forerunner to the trombone, which Le Roy played! I was amazed he could even think about that, let alone respond so quickly!

After the nurse threatened to call the doctor, Le Roy finally relented and allowed us to put the oxygen mask back on. But this truce didn't last for long, and I found myself bargaining with him:

If you will keep it on for a few seconds then I will let you keep it off for a while. However, the oxygen he was receiving was really allowing him to think faster and smarter. He started watching the wall clock to see how long I was making him wear it. Finally, I put the TV on, which distracted him enough that he kept the oxygen mask on most of the time.

I was really glad to see the doctor when he came on his early morning rounds. He told us the oxygen levels in his blood were high enough now he would only have to wear a nose air hose. Le Roy's color was good and his mind was as sharp as a tack! And he was feisty! Our friends Denny and Joanne came around eight to take me out for breakfast. When Denny asked Le Roy if he could "take his mom out for breakfast," he answered without losing a beat, "Yes, as long as you promise not to bring her back!" We laughed and laughed and knew he was recovering! How we needed that laughter!

Le Roy's radiation treatments were cancelled for that entire week. It was one of the best weeks he had during his entire treatment. The doctor told me that if I could administer his belly anti-coagulant shots, which he had to take for one week that he would be able to go home the next day. The thought of inserting a hypodermic needle in his abdominal region was not something I particularly wanted to do, but I was determined to do whatever it took if it meant he could come home. A hospital bed was ordered and delivered to our house, as it was now imperative that his head and upper body be elevated. So with an oxygen tank trailing behind us, we were released after five days and I drove us home.

Home Care Service was set up and a nurse came to the house every day to draw Le Roy's blood and check on oxygen levels. Coumadin thins the blood and helps to prevent blood clots. The abdominal shots would speed this process until the Coumadin had a chance to work through the liver in his system, which takes about a week. Now we had to be sure his blood didn't get too thin as there was still that risk of bleeding in the brain.

The week went by very quickly and we were amazed at how well his brain seemed to have recovered. Friends came over several times bringing dinners, eating with us and cleaning up the kitchen afterwards. How nice it was to relax for a moment and enjoy the laughter and visits with such dear friends. It seemed like old times. Even though Le Roy wasn't as sharp as he had been, nevertheless, it was a very special time – an oasis in this journey that had been fraught with dangers and a crisis at every turn.

Chapter 7

A Hope and Spirit Tested

"Have you not known? Have you not heard? The Lord is the everlasting God, the Creator of the ends of the earth. He does not faint or grow weary, his understanding is unsearchable. He gives power to the faint, and to him who has no might he increases strength. Even youths shall faint and be weary, and young men shall fall exhausted; but they who wait for the Lord shall renew their strength, they shall mount up with wings like eagles, they shall run and not be weary, they shall walk and not faint." (Is. 40:28-32)

Life with treatment resumed the following week and I immediately noticed a difference in Le Roy. The radiation zapped his strength and energy levels and he became sleepy and lethargic in the afternoons. The home nurse visits were discontinued and his blood was now checked at the oncology lab. He remained on oxygen, but he had made peace with the nose tubes, and except for some confusion and memory loss, seemed to be maintaining his level of brain processing. When we went for our weekly consultation, the oncologist seemed pleased at Le Roy's progress. My hope sprang high again as this progress report indicated that the tumor was shrinking and that some of his mental functioning might remain after treatments were completed.

Life slowed a bit and I started journaling once more. The Psalms continued to call out to me and they were a constant source of strength and hope. Each day it seemed I discovered a new verse that met my needs for that day and for that moment. They had become like personal friends and allowed me to open a dialogue with God that came as easy as talking with a friend. Some were like letters from God to me and many of these I copied into my Journal. There was healing through writing them down and inserting our names wherever it was appropriate. They became my prayers.

"Hear my cry, O God, listen to my prayer; from the end of the earth I call to thee, when my heart is faint. Lead thou me to the rock that is higher than I; for thou art my refuge, a strong tower against the enemy [tumor, illness, cancer, blood clots] *let me dwell in thy tent forever! Oh to be safe under the shelter of thy wings!"* (Psalm 61:1-4)

I knew I needed a strength and power outside myself. I needed to believe that God loved me as much as He did the people in the Bible. I needed to believe He was a personal God. Along with Psalms of hope, Psalms of praise for who God is and what He does and how He cares for us seemed to leap out at me, and I found enormous peace and comfort in reading them - a peace that truly did pass all understanding because I wasn't capable of creating that myself. I needed the mercy and power of God, and I knew medicine could only do so much.

"I give thee thanks, O Lord, with my whole heart; before the gods I sing thy praise; I bow down toward thy holy temple and give thanks to thy name for thy steadfast love and thy faithfulness; for thou hast exalted above everything thy name and thy word. On the day I called, thou didst answer me, my strength of soul thou didst increase." (Psalm 138:1-3)

It was now the end of March. Le Roy began to slow down as we took exercise walks up and down our long hallway, and he began to shuffle a little more every day. However, I still remained encouraged. And somehow I continued to believe that Le Roy would receive a miracle and live. Where does such a belief and hope come from?

Is it something we create to enable us to survive or is it a blessing God gives us to endure the unendurable - to be able to deny the unthinkable? I knew I wanted to believe that Le Roy would live.

My Journal:
JOY! For God has given me assurance that Le Roy will live! You have put your hope, faith and trust in Him who is greater than all. He gives you peace – a peace that doesn't come from denial instead of acceptance. Denial requires ongoing energy to keep it in place. Acceptance is open and unrestrictive, willing to experience pain.

But the daily progress log I was keeping was beginning to tell a different story and seemed to be in direct contrast to what I felt God was telling me in my spiritual walk. I was sure the assurance, peace and joy I was feeling was God's assurance that Le Roy would not only live, but would be totally healed!

How hard it must be for God to impart hope and faith and love to us to carry us through without our reading into that joy a false message of security. What God was doing and conveying was different than my perception of what the message was at the time. God was telling me, "I am with you – I will comfort you – Peace I give you even in the midst of turmoil and pain. You can even find joy in that! Because I am with you and will never leave you."

Later, I would re-read those journal entries and the quiet leading of the Holy Spirit would tell me that God wasn't assuring me Le Roy would be healed, but that God was assuring me He would be with us every minute, and that Le Roy would be made whole; but it would be when he went to live with His Savior. And that false perception took me on a journey of question and doubt and intense attack by the demons as I entered the final stages of Le Roy's life.

My Journal:
Last week I felt a strong assurance that Le Roy would be totally healed. I prayed several times about it. I asked God for assurance - for truth. I didn't want to believe something that wasn't so. I didn't want this to be a wish so strong of mine that I started thinking it was

from God. I told Him I could deal with the truth for He was the truth and He was reality. The assurance stayed.

My emotions have been up and down since then – believing in God, but not trusting myself. This morning in prayer, I again asked Him for assurance, because I wanted to be praying and believing in accordance with His Will, not mine. I feel I have to write it down so that when I'm not in prayer, when I am experiencing doubts that I can go read it. For isn't God more powerful than cancer, or anything? I believe this is God's confirmation and assurance to me that Le Roy will get well!

But it wasn't God's assurance – it was mine! It wasn't God telling me to write it down – it was my spirit doing that, trying to find hope in my feelings of peace and assurance in the only way I could bear to perceive it at the time. God knew I couldn't handle the whole truth all at once. He knew my heart. He wanted to fill it with hope and joy and love instead of the knowledge that Le Roy was going to die. God wasn't giving me assurance that Le Roy was going to live. He was giving me the assurance that He was going to be with us.

The progress log confirmed that he wasn't getting better. Le Roy was having more trouble picking up his feet to keep from stumbling on his walks and his shuffling gait became more pronounced. The doctors had adjusted his Dilantin levels and I was concerned this was causing the stumbling. But, he also was developing incontinence during the night. Already since the beginning of this month, he needed to get up two or more times a night to go to the bathroom. He had been sleeping in the hospital bed and sometimes he wasn't able to get up in time. This was occurring more frequently, and although he was supposed to sleep with his head elevated, there were times when, rather than change the sheets, I would just have him crawl into bed with me. Those were our favorite times because we could still cuddle and it seemed so good to go to sleep in his arms. I hated having him in the hospital bed away from me.

At times he was getting shaky and was sleeping more during the daytime. I tried to work on keeping his mind active. We worked on crossword puzzles, but he was no longer able to give me suggestions for words to use. Later in the week, the doctor decreased the Dilantin, although he didn't think the drug was causing the shuffling or shaking. But, based on Le Roy's ability to converse with him during consultations, the oncologist was still pleased about his progress. What a tribute to my husband's amazing mind.

Then one morning Le Roy fell as he came out of the bedroom. We had been having beautiful spring weather and he had wanted to wear his sandals. But they had a big, heavy tread and his shuffling gait caused him to trip on the rug and fall. In retrospect, I wonder if the fall was due more to the cancer and inflammation that was beginning to invade the motor portion of the brain. He hit his head on the wall, and even though he landed on the carpet instead of the tile entry floor, his right knee was bruised. I was scared, but he kept trying to reassure me that he was okay and that I shouldn't worry. He had a slight bruise on his forehead over the left eye. That morning I went to the cancer clinic with the volunteer driver who was taking Le Roy for his treatment, even though we had already seen the oncologist the day before. The oncologist checked for signs of a concussion and assured me he probably was okay. But he said I was to watch him closely for a few days.

I wrote in my progress log that the new Dilantin levels were not altering his shuffling gait and he was having trouble processing information again. He spent more time sleeping and he would be stiff and sore when he got up. We kept going for our little "walk-a-bouts" in the house to keep up his strength, but he began to complain about his right leg hurting.

My Journal:
Thank you God for bringing us safely through the night. Thank you for our answer to prayer every night. Thank you that Le Roy knows and feels your presence and healing touch.

All I could think of doing was to focus on hope and thank God for each little bit of help and progress I experienced no matter how small. On the 9th of April we visited his primary-care physician. Le Roy's oxygen levels had improved enough so that the oxygen he was obliged to be on since his return from his hospital stay was now eliminated except when he was walking around.

But the radiation treatments were really changing him, and he was becoming disoriented and tired. His right leg was swelling and getting so painful it was hard for him to stand. I became more and more concerned.

That night when I put him to bed, he talked about seeing Ward, a cousin that had been dead for over thirty years, and asked whether I had called his mother today. She too had died. That really shook me up. During the night Le Roy had to get up several times and I got very little sleep. I began to doubt the assurances that I believed God had given me about Le Roy getting better. I now felt he was dying and that the radiation was killing him.

We were nearing the end of his treatments with the focus of the radiation penetrating deeper in the brain. I was afraid that now the radiation was killing his good brain cells, and I was concerned that even if the cancer were eliminated, he would never return to his normal self. I began to doubt there even was a God and if there was a God, He had lied to me for I had prayed specifically that I wouldn't be given any false assurances. I was reaching burn out. It was a long night and a long morning.

Chapter 8

The Downward Slide

We were entering the twilight hours of Le Roy's life. His leg remained swollen and looked bruised. It was dawning on me that the fall might have had a greater impact on his knee than any of us realized. Because of his weakened condition from the radiation and cancer, normal healing would take longer. Things were happening so quickly and I was getting so tired, it was taking longer for me to connect the dots in the events. The bruised knee was impacting his whole leg, and his calf was swollen as well. Friends called from Arizona to pray with us and for us.

The oncologist thought the anti-inflammatory steroids were beginning to attack the muscles of the body and he lowered the levels of Decadron again. He suggested I massage his leg and keep him walking as much as possible - something that was getting harder and harder for both of us. I was exhausted and he was exhausted. I was trying to keep him upright even as he was trying to walk down those long hallways in our house. Even though he had the support of the walker, it would have been impossible for me to help him back up should he fall, and that was always a very real possibility.

It was Holy week and my journal recorded the struggle I was in.

My Journal:
I am in a battle and last night the demons won. As I put Le Roy to bed and watched as he struggled with the weakness and pain in his left leg and knee, I felt scared. Even when I read Psalm 18, inserting our names with God fighting the cancer, I worried - and the tears keep coming. I asked Le Roy if he wanted to stop the treatments. And he said no.

Le Roy talks about seeing a cousin who has been dead for years, and asked if I had called his mother and confused me with his first wife from over 43 years earlier. We both thought it was the result of the radiation. As I prayed with him it soothed and quieted my anxiety enough for me to go to sleep. But at 3 or 4 in the morning I woke up with Le Roy trying to get out of bed to go to the bathroom. He was in such pain. Again, I felt he was dying and I felt betrayed.

After tucking him back into bed, I lay awake thinking that God must have lied to me. My assurance for complete healing was replaced with assurance that he was going to die. How could this be, when God had repeatedly given me His assurance? Maybe there wasn't even a God. I crawled into the hospital bed with Le Roy, clinging to his warmth and willing myself to tolerate the back pain from a fused back so I could stay there with him. Finally, the alarm went off and I got up to give him his pill.

I lay down for a while, then got up again and tried to find some comfort in one of my Bible books. I could not. I felt wasted - a wasteland - and I read and reread what I had written about the assurances. Maybe it was just the demons. Maybe he wasn't going to die. Maybe. . . I stopped thinking and instead resolved to make each moment count with Le Roy, and once more went back to bed with him a little while before we had to get up. Later that day I went with him to his treatment so I could ask the doctor about his leg. He felt the swelling and pain wasn't caused by the radiation, but rather the steroids, which he was going to reduce once more. I wanted to cheer! It was reversible! It wasn't the cancer or the radiation!

I felt rejuvenated once more - he might be okay. He was going to be okay! I prayed and told God I was too tired and weak to be tested any more. But demons don't come from God. And I am battle worn and scarred and can only ask simply, and not with much feeling or conviction, God please carry me.

My emotions were up and down from one extreme to another, and what little energy levels I had rose and fell with them. The incontinence at nighttime was getting worse and I often couldn't wake up in time to get him to the bathroom. He fell once when he struggled to get up out of his hospital bed before I could wake up, and I was so worried he would hurt himself. His brain just was not functioning properly. And I was completely worn out. Things were happening so quickly and were so unpredictable. There was no way to know how to plan.

My Journal:
April 12th. This is Le Roy's last day of radiation. His mind and body are broken. He is developing a cough that won't go away. I am broken, too, in spirit. Should he have this last treatment or will it push him over the edge? But if not, will it be the treatment that didn't kill all the cancer cells? How stupid and naive I am to think that the radiation would be any less harsh on him than chemo. Yet what choice did we have? He had needed treatment - immediately.

I have lifted my broken spirit to God. I have re-read the assurance passages. I no longer know if they were assurances. I prayed Psalm 143 as I read it from "The Message" by Eugene Peterson: ". . . I sat there in despair, my spirit draining away, my heart heavy, like lead. I remembered the old days, went over all you've done, pondered the ways you've worked, stretched out my hands to you, as thirsty for you as a desert thirsty for rain. Hurry with your answer, God! I'm nearly at the end of my rope . . ." The outcome really is up to God. I can only do the best I can to care for Le Roy and give him all the love I have and all the strength I can muster. I desperately miss my Christian friends and wish they were here.

Maundy Thursday Le Roy came home from the cancer clinic with his face mask and a diploma of treatment completion signed by everyone in the clinic. He had graduated. I didn't know whether to jump for joy or weep. Again a friend from Arizona called and prayed with me. How precious were those prayers, as I was too tired to hope, cry or pray.

Most of that day Le Roy just sat in his recliner resting and napping. I finished some housecleaning and checked on him frequently to see if he needed to go to the bathroom. He was now very unsteady on his feet. He was losing control of his physical body. The incontinence that occurred during the night was now happening in the daytime. It shook me to the core.

My Journal:
It is Good Friday - the day Jesus died on the cross. I feel like I have been going through a Holy Week in microcosm. How did Jesus do it?

Yesterday I had reached a point of total despair again. But once more I had to put my faith in "Thy Will be done." Again Frank called from Tucson and prayed with me over the phone. What a blessing.

Last night Le Roy and I slept together in our own bed. How good it was to hold his hand all night and know he was right there beside me instead of the hospital bed across the room. We woke at four for a bathroom break, but then was able to go back to sleep and slept until 8:45. It was so nice to get some rest! Le Roy had the beginning of hiccups, but they stopped. I had his legs elevated. We left his oxygen on because he was having periods of coughing.

When we awoke, Le Roy's leg and foot seemed less swollen. Maybe keeping it elevated night and day was finally helping. He was even able to walk without pain medications and he seemed to be brighter. Good Friday. Maybe on Easter Sunday we would experience a resurrection!

God's message for me that day came from I Kings 19:4. Even Elijah after winning a great victory over pagan prophets fled the next day in despair because Queen Jezebel threatened to have him killed. Exhausted and depressed, Elijah asked God to take his life. As God gently led Elijah out of his darkness, so God is gently leading me. It seemed God was trying to get through to me that I should just spend as much quality time with Le Roy as possible and don't worry about the outcome.

On Saturday things got worse again. I was up three times with Le Roy during the night. He remained disoriented. I could tell he was trying so hard to make his mind work but it just couldn't respond. I use the wheelchair to move him almost all the time now except when we try to exercise a little by walking down the hall with his walker. It was a beautiful sunny day and I took him outside to enjoy the warm weather. Maybe it would lift our spirits as well. That night after praying together he told me he thought his relatives were doing this to him. And then he said he believed he was dying. It pierced my heart and I tried to reassure him that he was getting well. But he knew at some level that he wasn't.

Until now when we talked about what was happening, Le Roy could only say that he felt okay. He knew he was getting treatment, but he could not process the fact that this was very serious because he didn't feel sick. Because the tumor was in his cerebral cortex, his ability to process everything that was happening was limited. But awareness was sinking in to a new level.

I had Le Roy sleep with me now at night instead of the hospital bed because I just couldn't risk his falling and getting hurt. I couldn't leave him for even a few minutes. One night when I ran to the laundry room to get another pair of pajamas, he tried to walk by himself and fell. I hold onto his pajamas in bed so I can wake up as soon as he tries to get out of bed.

While Saturday had been sunny and warm, Easter Sunday was cold, gray and dreary. I struggled to help Le Roy get dressed and shaved. He had regressed again and could no longer do these simple every day tasks. Our daughter and her family came to share dinner with us. Our sons, unable to be there with us, called and talked to both of us. Le Roy slept most of the day. I remember reading a psalm of praise so we could remain upbeat.

My Journal:
I can't read scriptures. My mind is in turmoil. My devotional for today was Gal. 2:20 which said, "I am crucified with Christ." I did not want to be crucified with Christ. It had no comfort for me today.

That night things got even worse. Le Roy had become so disoriented and his thinking so muddled it seemed like he was sinking into oblivion. I felt as low as I could possibly get. I was bereft: spiritually, emotionally and physically. I was fighting a heavy spiritual battle and my faith was badly shaken. I felt that God had forsaken me and I had to resist the temptation to even believe there might not be a God, for I knew there was.

Le Roy's incontinence was increasing during the daytime. I called the Cancer Clinic to get his Dexadron medication reduced because he was beginning to have tremors. The oncologist told me that was not a good sign and said the symptoms indicated that Le Roy's tumor had not shrunk very much. He scheduled an MRI on Thursday of that week to see how much effect the radiation had on the tumor.

My Journal:
I have been doing everything in my power to help bring about healing for Le Roy. But, I can't heal him – only God can. But I can use my energy to help him in his journey walking closer to our God.

Today I accept the fact that he is dying. I got on my knees and prayed the prayer I prayed for our son Don so many years ago. But that prayer was for strength to raise him - strength for a beginning. This prayer was also acceptance - but letting go - in dying.

I could no longer hope for a recovery. I knew I had to let Le Roy go. And I felt compelled to get on my knees beside my bed and pray that prayer to God. Somehow it was a measure of a solemn release and commitment. I told God that He could take him, that His Will be done, and that I was letting him go. I do not know how I was able to pray that prayer because I wanted him to live with every fiber of my being. Besides my children, Le Roy was everything to me.

Years ago, I had prayed for the future of our ten-month old son, Don, after bringing him home from the Oregon Medical School Hospital where he had spent five days of intensive testing. He had been diagnosed a-mi-tonic quadriplegic. When we brought him home, I knew I had to get on my knees to pray for him and for us.

As a young girl I used to kneel by my bed at night to say my prayers. But as a young adult I said my prayers in the comfort of my chair.

Then, as now, I knew this prayer could only be said on my knees. When I prayed for my son I instinctively knew I could not ask God to remove the condition he had or even ask for a miracle to have him healed. I could only pray that we would have the strength to make our son's life as normal and happy as possible.

And God had answered that prayer. Although he wasn't healed, neither was he a-mi-tonic quadriplegic. He had been born with muscle weaknesses and lacked some of the necessary neck muscles to hold up his head. But with braces and an operation that fused part of his back when he reached puberty, he went on to become a talented and successful commercial artist who lived and worked in Los Angeles.

But this time, I knew my prayer was going to result in an ending. I really was giving Le Roy to God in the most literal sense. I felt God was asking me to accept the fact that he was dying. Somehow in that acceptance I began to release the endless tension of hope and no hope that was destroying me.

In the days that followed, Le Roy would have good days when he seemed to be coming out of his fog and I could read e-mails and letters to him. I would give him photo albums of his college students and his bands and I could tell he really enjoyed looking at the pictures. Sometimes it seemed his health improved so much that when our sons would call it was hard not to have some hope. Both our sons were still optimistic despite what the doctor had told us.

But I was cautioning myself not to become so hopeful that I would come crashing down. It did seem strange that now when I had finally given up, accepting the inevitable, other people were still feeling that Le Roy was going to get well.

My Journal:
Frank called and after praying again with him, Le Roy rallied so much it was hard not to feel hope rise again. But I am doing my best not to raise my hopes. Twice his incontinence won over waking up. I can no longer get him up and to the bathroom by myself. This morning I read II Cor. 12:9 "My grace is sufficient for you, for my

power is made perfect in weakness." And I understand at a new level that God wants me to put my entire faith in Him - not just to make Le Roy well, but because that is where I belong.

"But He knows the way that I take; when he has tried me, I will come forth as gold." (Job 23: 10) My focus is no longer "will Le Roy get well." My focus is to put my entire trust in God - whatever the outcome - period!

But while I could write these words, living them was something totally different. However, I no longer struggled with Le Roy's destiny. I was able to let go and in that letting go, found comfort and peace.

That wonderful, intelligent, logical brain of Le Roy's no longer was able to send the messages needed for the body to respond. He rarely talked. How I missed his humor that made our life so enjoyable. How I longed to talk to him about what was going on. But not only was he unable to control his body, neither was he able to mindfully share what was happening to him.

The incontinence increased. It was impossible to get him to the bathroom, and sheets and pajamas were constantly being changed. It had all happened so rapidly I didn't even have time to ask someone to get some adult diapers. All our friends had been out of town for some time, my boys were unavailable in different states, and my daughter and her husband struggled to keep afloat with the demands of a premature baby. I was on my own and had been for some time. I wasn't even aware how long. But about the time the tumor had escalated events to crisis proportion again, a neighborhood acquaintance stopped by to bring us a dinner and she asked if there was anything she could do. I quickly asked her to go to the store with a list of what I needed.

At times it seemed we would come out of a crisis long enough to rest for a day or two. I remember early one morning how nice it was to simply enjoy snuggling with him for a little while before I had to get up and give him his pills. He could still snuggle, even though I had to help put his arms around me. I no longer kept him in the hospital bed. At those fleeting but special moments it was hard to believe that he really was dying. Everything within me shouted, "No, he isn't going to die. He is going to live."

Where does that kind of hope come from? Although these times were few, it seemed we lived a lifetime in them, soaking up those precious moments as though they give us strength to live. But the evidence of his dying was always there all around me. Once or twice a day I still tried to help him walk a little. But his legs just wouldn't allow it.

On Friday, April 20th, his primary care physician called and told us the MRI report indicated that although there was no new growth, there was little shrinkage of the tumor and there was swelling around the motor area of the brain. That was probably why Le Roy was having such difficulty standing and would suddenly lose control of his legs when walking. Even with all the preparation in my mind about letting him go, I felt devastated. I hadn't realized at some level I was still hoping for a miracle.

Chapter 9

Walking Through the Valley

"Even though I walk through the valley of the shadow of death, I fear no evil; for thou art with me; thy rod and thy staff, they comfort me." (Psalm 23:4)

The last weekend in April our son Bob drove up from Portland. It was a good weekend. Le Roy was alert, he was able to walk a little unaided, he joked with us at the dinner table and he just seemed to be himself. It was to be the last weekend where he was aware of what was happening. Although we didn't realize it yet, we were rapidly moving towards the final days and hours of Le Roy's life.

Le Roy's cognitive levels remained high while our son was with us, and we even thought his body was getting stronger. But I was so afraid to get my hopes up. Our son left knowing at some level that it was the last time he would be able to interact with his dad.

It was so difficult to watch Bob leave early Sunday afternoon, and both Le Roy and I felt very empty and alone. Although neither of us could speak about it, I could see it in his face. Our friends, Skip and Barbara, came over to see us twice that day. I remember Le Roy insisting on going to the door each time to say goodbye to them. He was still a host, not a dying man, and even though he had to get out of his recliner and into his wheelchair he insisted on going to the door. At such moments, I don't think he was aware of just how ill he was.

The next day, he took a 180 degree turn backwards. Although most of the day he was awake, his cognitive and emotional capacity and muscle control faded incredibly by evening. While his body seemed stronger over the weekend, today he had become very unsteady and it was very difficult to get him out of his recliner. The recliner had been his daytime "bed" as it was very comfortable for him.

That night I had a difficult time getting him into his wheelchair and into bed. He tried so hard to help in the process, but his brain just wouldn't respond to his wishes. By the time we made it to bed, I was exhausted. How could one day be so dramatically different from the day before? I lay there and read some Psalms and prayed together with him. While the weekend had been sunny and hopeful, the world was once again gray and foreboding.

When Le Roy fell asleep, I stayed awake. I tried so hard not to hold onto any hope of recovery. Hope had now become a thing to fear; a dreaded dragon that reared its ugly head and demolished me with its cheap, false message.

My Journal:
I am struggling to accept more and more fully that there is no miracle of recovery for Le Roy and me. Emotions of any kind are too painful – too draining. Acceptance now must require no feeling or I won't be able to care for Le Roy as I'd like. Emotions take too much energy. They used to energize. But now they cut me to pieces. I feel as though I have been beaten, whipped and hung on my own cross. I want to pray the same prayer as Jesus: "Father, Father, why have you forsaken me?" and "Father, if there is any other way than drinking this cup. . ." I feel compelled to pray, "Father into Thy Hands I commit my Spirit." But when I say it, I find no peace – just deadness. I feel dead inside. Life without hope is death. Oh God, please help me.

Hope has become like the devil – enticing – encouraging – sweet, wonderful joy and then as you let yourself become seduced you see instead its ugly head. It's just a sham. There has never been any hope. The woman at the driver's license office when I went in to get Le Roy's disabled sticker told me about her cousin who had a Glioblastnoma. He is still alive after three years! Hope! It keeps raising its ugly head. And when I buy into it, I get hurt.

One of the devotionals for this week was written by Mrs. Charles E. Cowman who told a story about how birds got their wings. The fable said that in the beginning birds had beautiful feathers and sweet voices, but they didn't have any wings and could not fly. They could sing beautiful songs, but they could not soar in the air. So God made them wings. When He placed them down before the wingless birds, He said: "Take up these burdens and bear them."

At first the birds hesitated. But soon they placed the wings on their shoulders. The load seemed heavy and hard to bear at first, but as they continued to carry these "burdens," the wings grew onto their bodies and they discovered how to use them. When they did, they lifted them into the air. The "burdens" had become wings. The moral of the fable was that we, too, are wingless birds and our burdens are the wings that will enable us to soar and fly. The scripture for that day was Isaiah 40: 31: *"They shall mount up with wings as eagles."*

The story had an impact on me. All week I had been writing about hope and God and my struggle to believe and my desire for Le Roy to live.

My Journal:
It's no good! I cannot not hope! I cannot not believe! Without hope I am dead. Without God there is no life. I feel dead – a dead person trying to live who is carrying all his burdens like the birds with wings who weren't using them – the wings that were just burdens. Each burden – job – responsibility becomes a stone – bigger – heavier. But it doesn't totally crush you – it just continues to weigh you down. The struggle goes on. And isn't that hell – hell on earth! Hell anywhere.

Then does hope come from the devil to raise us up and then crush us? No it really can't be. Hope is the effort to fly with wings not yet grown. If I don't hope – don't try – don't struggle, there will never be the possibility of flying. I cannot live without hope. If I get bruised and bloodied because of it, so be it. But to live without hope is worse than struggling – flapping wings that don't take you anywhere. Just like pushing against a stone, whether it moves or not, you become strong. By flapping our wings they attach themselves securely and begin to carry us. I want to soar like the eagles. I always have. I just never knew it required such a workout to accomplish it.

Hope! It is a gift I cannot refuse. Belief. It is the assumption that God catches you when reality doesn't match your hopes and you begin to fall. You may not be aware of being caught and held safely because the terror of falling is too great. But God is there regardless of how you feel, like the parachute keeping a skydiver from plummeting to earth. A skydiver has learned to turn his fear of falling into a heady joy of floating. When reality has dashed my hope, how do I turn my fear of falling into floating?

In order to fly, you have to exercise your wings. In order to fly you have to be willing to fall and "let go" of your fear of heights, "let go" and free fall – spreading your arms so you can catch the updrafts and float. In order to fly, you must have hope. Hope can energize. It seeks new solutions, as you learn from crashes what to do and what not to do. Fear grounds you – makes you miserable, resentful, blaming. Fear eats you up and spits you out in the garbage dump! Hope reaches upward. Fear drives you down into the ground. Hope is the wings that will enable me to fly.

I don't see Le Roy dying – even when I was trying to beat Hope to death. How far he will come in his recovery, I don't know. Is it possible for him to regain all his faculties? Yes, it is - because with God nothing is impossible. The question remains, am I willing to allow such hope? Yes, I believe I am. But I won't crash and burn when all signs tell me he is dying. I will just let my wings carry me in a float until I can catch the next updraft!

We were entering the last phases of Le Roy's life. One night I had to get up four times. It was getting more and more difficult to handle him. He would wake up and want to go to the bathroom by himself. Somehow I had to keep him there by the bed and help him use the urinal instead. The adult pampers were not easy to take off or re-apply. He wanted to do the work himself, but he couldn't.

The last time when I had to get up I was so tired I lost my patience with him and got cross. He stopped trying to help me. I felt horrible afterwards, devastated that I had allowed myself to speak crossly to him. The next day when I wrote about the incident in my journal, I wept and without being able to tell him for he no longer was aware of what was happening to him, I asked him to forgive me. *"Forgive me, Le Roy, for getting cross with you. I love you so much!"*

That last week spent in our home was a blur. Calling hospice was a reality that the end was near. They didn't have any hospice people available to help me either on a full time or part time basis. They could only send me a nurse once a day to administer medications or give advice. I hired an aide from an outside agency to assist me in the mornings, but it did not give me any relief for the night. The struggle to get Le Roy from his recliner to a wheelchair to take him to the bathroom or put him to bed was getting more difficult and dangerous. One night I asked the elderly couple who lived across the street from me to assist me in putting him to bed. I was so afraid he would fall and I would not be able to pick him up. Just having them hold the wheelchair steady while I got him up and into it was a big help.

Hospice ordered another hospital bed for the kitchen and the nurse installed a catheter. The last weekend home I was finally able to hire a caretaker to spend the night so I could try and get some sleep. It was important that he not be left alone because although he was no longer communicating and seemed to be totally unaware of what was happening, at some level he was still trying to live life as usual and without warning he would try to get up on his own.

But the time had arrived when I needed more than night time help or a few hours during the day. I could no longer handle him at all. His body wouldn't respond to whatever commands his brain tried to give. There was no alternative. He would have to go into a care facility. I called Hospice and they ordered an ambulance to take him there. On the way I tried to tell Le Roy what I was seeing as we went along. But he was no longer able to respond. He was placed in a section of the facility that Hospice used for dying patients.

After they had him settled in, I went back home, but warned the nurses that he would try to get up on his own. They didn't believe he could do that since he seemed like someone in a coma and was dead weight when they moved him. They were very surprised when the triggering device they attached to his pajamas went off during the night and before they were able to reach the room he already was sitting up and trying to get out of bed.

I was determined not to leave him again. Our wonderful neighbors said they would take care of our little dog. I packed my bag and returned to the care facility and stayed with him until he died. He was no longer visibly cognizant of my presence, but I knew at some level he knew I was there. The care facility found a recliner and placed it beside his bed where I stayed day and night. I only left for short periods when family or friends would come and take me out for a meal. I held his hand while I slept at night and during the day.

I brought a small CD player from home and played his music: the big bands – Frank Sinatra – trombone music. The songs on the CD seemed to speak to us about our lives and what was happening to us at that moment: "You are the Sunshine of my life," and "What Now My love," and "You Will Be My Music." The final song, "My Way," seemed to speak of Le Roy's life. He didn't follow the crowd. He didn't do things just because everyone else did them. He lived by his principles. He was responsible for his actions on a personal level and in his professional life. He did it "his way," not the world's way! Sometimes I would lie on top of the bed beside him and cradle his head on my shoulder and I knew at some level he was hearing the music I was playing for him. I had the feeling that his toes were moving to the beat.

But my darling - the love of my life - was dying. The moment finally came when I was told he no longer could eat or swallow and I had to make the decision either to withhold food and water or keep him physically alive with feeding tubes and IVs which only prohibit the body from dying. We both had Living Wills and had never wanted to be hooked up to machines or kept alive beyond our time to die. Honoring that was so difficult because I wanted to extend his life as long as possible. But I had to honor his wishes just as I would want others to honor mine.

As hard as it was, I made the decision quickly. I was determined to just love him as much as possible with every ounce of energy left in me. The day before he died, the hospice nurse told me she had never experienced so much love in a dying room from all his friends and family.

My part of this journey through the valley of the shadow of death was nearing an end. The night he was going to die I knew deep down I couldn't hold his hand anymore because I was keeping him here and it was time for him to go. But I couldn't just remove my hand from him. So instead of holding his hand, I simply laid my hand on his arm. And around 1:15 in the morning I awoke to his long labored breathing. And I knew.

I got up and sat beside him, took his hand, and while rocking back and forth tried to comfort him and myself. With a heart that was breaking, I told him it was okay for him to go. I had to stay, but he had to go and I was going to be okay. And as I rocked and silently wept, I kept telling him how much I loved him, but he had to go to his heavenly home now – he could no longer stay. I knew I wasn't holding him back any more and it was okay to hold his hand – that beautiful hand that had held his trombone and played such sweet music. His last breaths were long and labored with long stretches of time in between. Then finally, he left me, his last breath a long, slow sigh. He was gone.

It is over. It is finished. I did not feel his spirit leave, but I had been given a vision of him the day before of him entering heaven, radiant and happy, letting me know he no longer needed his old body. He had a new one. I thanked God for that last beautiful gift.

God, I know you have touched many lives with the death of Le Roy. There was a purpose. There was a reason. And thank you, God, for giving him to me for 43 years! I have been blessed, even as my heart is breaking and I feel like I have died too.

Final E-Mail
Tuesday, May 8, 2001 - 3:44 PM

This is to let everyone know that Le Roy passed away at 1:45 this morning May 8th. He died peacefully and was in no pain. We fought a valiant fight, but he is now at home with his Heavenly Father and we are all at peace.

Thanks for your prayers. God is holding us in the palm of his hand and we find comfort and joy in the midst of our sorrow. What a GREAT GUY he was!!

Love,
Marlene

PART TWO

"Draw near to God and he will draw near to you." (James 4:8)

MY JOURNEY ALONE

Chapter 10

Walking Alone

What do you feel when someone you love has just died? Numb. You don't feel; you go through the motions – even emotional responses to friends and family are superficial – habits that continue without feeling. You can laugh, enjoy their company, and yet, it is as though you were fractured – split – and another you is doing these things. The real you cannot feel.

Our children couldn't stay with me the night Le Roy died, even though they all knew the end was near. Our friends had been concerned when they had left the evening before and asked the nurse to contact them if Le Roy passed away during the night. The nurse called them and I called each of my children. It was 1:45 in the morning. Elizabeth was awake. She knew.

I could no longer cry. I had cried while he was dying and now all that remained was emptiness. One of the staff at the care center whom I hardly knew came into the room with tears streaming down her face to tell me how sorry she was. I thanked her, touched by her genuine sympathy, and found myself reaching out to console her. I packed Le Roy's things and mine and when Frank arrived, assured him I could drive my car home. He followed me to be sure I got home safely.

I opened the sunroof of my car and felt the cold night air blow on my face and in my hair. I saw the stars. Months later, my daughter asked how I felt driving home after Dad had died. Numb. I could no longer feel. A part of me had also died. Another part functioned by rote. I tried to envision Le Roy there in the stars. But I couldn't.

When you lose someone you love so much it's as though you become mortally wounded. The person you used to be no longer exists. I became a walking zombie who moved and functioned, ate and visited with friends, but who was dead inside. There was a large wound, a huge hole in my heart and being. Oh, you couldn't see it. But it was there and I felt the essence of my life ooze away through it while my body and mind frantically tried to survive, frantically tried to cauterize the wound and numb the pain.

We are programmed for survival. When you experience a trauma the brain releases chemicals, analgesics, to numb pain. Your emotional response is decreased. There is a separation, a containment of what you are feeling from what you are experiencing until at some point those pent up emotions demand release. It takes a lot of energy to keep unprocessed emotions in check. If they are kept buried and denied for a long period of time, they often begin to emerge in unhealthy and negative ways.

We do not want to feel pain and will go to great lengths to avoid experiencing it. We take all kinds of pills to relieve our physical pain. But there is no magic pill to relieve the emotional pain. There is no way to get beyond emotional and psychological pain except to go through it. There is no way to mourn the loss of a loved one except to allow yourself to feel the pain. You may be able to shove it aside for a while, ignore it, sidestep it, and keep so busy there isn't time for it, but sooner or later, your loss and pain will demand your attention. You can only contain it for so long. However painful, as you allow yourself to grieve something positive and constructive can happen. Something good can come out of the worst of tragedies.

That is where I found myself after Le Roy had died. I had walked with him through the valley of the shadow of death until I had to let go of his hand; only he could continue his walk to be with our Lord. But I still felt I was there within that long, dark valley with no promise of sunshine or a future. I felt I had no place to go.

And so my journey began - alone. In order to get out of that long, dark valley I needed to allow the numbness to recede so I could move towards healing. But as I did, everything inside of me screamed "No. No, I don't want to go on alone." This was a pain no medication could numb. This was greater than any physical pain I had ever experienced.

On May 15th I started journaling again. It was my way of surviving. It was my way to release the pain.

My Journal:

A new chapter. So much has happened – crisis after crisis rolling over us like waves from an angry ocean. Maybe as I start this new chapter in my life, a new beginning that I never wanted, I will be able to record more of the layers and layers of thoughts and feelings about this past four month journey. One moment he was here – the next he was gone. He is gone! Le Roy is gone! He has died. The tumor has taken my wonderful husband. How do you absorb that reality?

As I write, a part of me recoils and my stomach flip-flops and wants to be sick. I think maybe I am still suspended, held up in prayer, insulated from pain by the love of my friends and family. But I know at some point I will acutely feel the pain. And I also know God will be there covering that pain with a blanket of His love.

There have been so many blessings along the way. God has blessed me by giving Le Roy to me for all those years. He blessed me by extending Le Roy's life those extra four months. Le Roy would have hated having only half a mind. So without complete healing, it is a blessing that God took him home.

Arizona is calling. [Before Le Roy got sick we had visited Arizona several times and we were planning to build a small home in Tucson where we could spend our winters in the sun.] *I want to wake up to sunshine and warmth, and eat outdoors on a patio year round. But I also want to remain connected and close to Elizabeth and be an active part in Aria's life as she grows up. God, how will you work all this out?*

What a wonderful memorial service we had in Portland. We had lived so many years in Portland and knew so many people; I wanted to have a memorial service there as well as here at Salem Lutheran. The chapel at Lewis & Clark College was beautiful as was the campus. It was a warm, sunny day with the scent of bursting spring flowers and new life everywhere. People – former teachers, colleagues, students and friends - spoke for over an hour about how Le Roy had impacted their lives. Fellow musicians and colleagues played. What a tribute! And my stay with John and Carol afterwards was so healing.

As I wrote in my journal every day, my thoughts seemed fragmented and tumbled from event to event within a single entry. I would write about his death, then where I was going to live, and then the pull of my newest granddaughter, Aria. She would never get to know her grandfather. And I would weep. I felt so needy. I felt so alone. I wanted to have a direction. But there was no roadmap. I drew as close to God as I knew how to receive a comfort not even loving friends and family could give me. My world had shut down, but I was still forced to exist in it.

My Journal:
Yesterday was horrible! I could only endure half a day in my home office. I used to love working there, studying, writing, preparing for workshops and classes. I was always organized and proficient. But now it took an hour to sort through papers on my desk. I couldn't wait to get out of the house. I was extremely dismayed at how grief-stricken I was all day. I wanted to run. I wanted to do anything to get away from the pain.

I would drive to Seattle and spend time with Elizabeth and Aria. I hoped that being with her would help me feel less alone and help deal with the loss. But my grief followed me everywhere I went. Elizabeth and I held each other as we cried. Holding and cuddling my new granddaughter gave me a few moments of joy.
But when I returned home, the pain resumed. I have always been a "people person" and our home was always full of laughter and conversations. Even in our quiet solitude times, it was enough to know that Le Roy was there in his office or practicing or would be arriving home at some time. But now, the reality that he would never again be physically present was overwhelming.

My Journal:
I hate being alone. But I can't fathom anyone else taking his place. Oh God, isn't there an easier way to get through the pain of being alone? Truly alone? Oh, I will have my friends and family, but no longer the intimacy, the comforting sense that I don't have to face each new day alone – all the decisions. There will be no one to take me in his arms where I can just let go, give and receive comfort and share the load. Dear God, please spare me days like yesterday. I know I can't run away from the pain or stuff it or ignore it, but please help me find ways to make it easier to endure!

But there is no easy way to get through grief and loss. Some days will seem as though they will never end and others will seem like life is returning to normal. There are so many layers of loss. In the days and months ahead I not only grieved the man I loved so much, but also grieved the loss of my identity within that relationship, grieved the loss of being a couple and grieved the loss of a future as well. For marriage had been such a large part of my life – a part of who I was. And I could not imagine anyone taking his place.

My Journal:
As I look out this morning on gray skies, I am acutely aware of its effect on me emotionally. But as I immerse myself in Hannah Smith's writings and 1st John, I find comfort.

What really helped me through those early days and next two years, besides the wonderful support of my pastor, church, friends and family, was the time I spent each morning reading, writing and talking to a God who drew very near to me. As had happened during the time Le Roy was ill, it seemed that whenever I opened my Bible, God was pointing out scripture verses that were going to touch me in some way that day, that moment.

Another book that became like a second Bible to me during this time was, "The God of All Comfort" written by Hannah Whitall Smith over a hundred years ago. My wonderful neighbor, Shirlee, had brought it over to me when Le Roy was ill. I'm sure it was God who prompted her to give it to me, for surely God knew I needed to hear the words Hannah Smith wrote, so many years ago, about how very much God loves us. Love. How I needed to hear again that God loved and cared about me personally as much as my friends did.

Chapter 11

Details and More Details

*T*hose early weeks demanded I pay attention to all the paperwork that changed our names from a "we" to an "I." Every bank, every institution had its own procedure for making this happen, and they all wanted original death certificates, not copies. I was still numbed by shock and my capacity to think was greatly diminished. And yet, the decisions you are required to make have long-term consequences.

Le Roy had always taken care of our investments. And while he always saw to it that I understood what we had and what we were doing, it still was his area of expertise and I had happily let him take care of it. Although I thought I knew what had to be done in the eventuality that he died first, I was surprised at how little I really did know, the depth of vocabulary and knowledge that I lacked and how much I had to rely on the decent people who do work at such institutions to help me. My ability to work for any length of time in my office was minimal compared to what I had always been able to do in the past. I went from a highly organized, energized person to someone who struggled to move and think and function. Gradually I got through all the paperwork.

This was also a time to re-assess my financial situation. Le Roy and I had always made decisions together, and now I was painfully aware that I would be making them alone. I felt very vulnerable because I knew that intense emotions and grief can keep a person from thinking rationally. I was fortunate, however, to have a number of highly qualified, trusted friends whom I could go to for advice. They became my mentors.

When Le Roy was getting treatment for his tumor, I put our house up for sale because we had talked about building a smaller home and splitting our time between Washington in the summer and Arizona in the winter. During that window of time when it seemed as though he was going to survive and he was able to think, we talked about continuing with those plans. A lot we had previously looked at came on the market and I started sketching out a new house design. But when his health began to deteriorate again, the house was taken off the market and any thoughts about the future were shelved.

Now I had to think again about what I wanted to do. It was a big house, and expenses were a concern. General wisdom says do not make a major move for at least a year after the death of your spouse and it is good advice. Later that summer and fall, my journal entries reflected the conflict I was in about what to do and where I should live.

My Journal:
Should I stay within the community I now lived in? Should I move closer to my daughter and son-in-law? Should I think about moving to Arizona where the sun could help bolster my spirits? Should I simply move into an apartment and consider my entertaining days finished? If I stayed in my current home, would I be able to keep up the maintenance and handle the cost?

It was too early in the grieving process; the emotions were too raw to see any kind of positive future for myself. If my life was over, shouldn't the house be sold too? It only held memories – but they were memories I treasured. I prayed and struggled to find answers.

My Journal:
Today is rainy, cold and gray. And I wonder where do I go from here? My devotional this morning talks about purpose and priorities – asking God questions of purpose. What do you want me to do, God, with my remaining years? When I was at my friend's home last night,

I had such a good time. I must stay connected to my friends and start making more. I must create a life separate from my children even if that takes me farther away from them. It would be so easy to attach myself to their lives, and that could happen so subtly, but it would destroy the wonderful relationship I have with them. God, help me with this. Where will I live? What do you want me to do?

As part of this transition from "we" to "I," at some point I needed to remove some of his things from the house. In the beginning, I gave as many things away as I could and was comforted in the fact that it was a continuation of Le Roy in the process. The kids of course could have whatever they wanted. Bob took his dad's synthesizer and some music. Elizabeth and Gene were given his telescope. A violin that Le Roy's dad had made went to Bob and another one was saved for Aria when she grew up. Don chose some personal articles. He didn't want very much. He clung to his memories. Other things they wanted me to save for them.

At some point I realized it was time to remove Le Roy's personal effects from the bathroom drawers. I was unprepared for the emotional impact that had on me. It felt like a lead ball had hit me in the pit of my stomach. Many of the items had to be thrown away, and I felt as though I was discarding Le Roy in the process. It took all my strength to finish what would ordinarily be such a simple job. I was exhausted after emptying those few drawers in the bathroom.

Except for some of his best clothes which I had given to my sons and personal friends, it was much later before I could actually dispose of the rest. Removing everything was like finalizing an ending I didn't want to make. There was a part deep down inside of me that wanted to believe he would return. It was another layer of reality that I still had to go through. I kept his favorite leather jacket and the King trombone that he had made specifically for him early in his career. I still have them.

My Journal:
"I'm being asked to let go of so much, Le Roy, and it's hard. I had to let go of you and that was the hardest. I think I will have to let go of the beautiful house we designed and built together. I need to let

go of all your things – the things that were a part of your life – the things you loved and took such good care of. I need to let go of the life we had together. I can no longer live it as though you were here by my side. And I know I need to let go of my kids, in some sense too, because it will be the only way I can start creating my own life. I don't want to put a burden on them to meet my emotional needs. And yet, I want to be there if they need me and I need to be close enough if I need them.

"And now what, Le Roy? I feel naked and empty. I've let go of my treasures – for you and my kids are my treasures. How do I create a new beginning? How does one let go of a life time relationship of meaning and commitment? To what? Our friends gather around me at Bible study and comfort me when I cry and pray for me. I have their warmth and love, but when I return home, I am alone again. I'm a baby at this. I have to take baby steps. And I guess I have to believe that My Heavenly Father will be there to catch me when I stumble and fall."

Life doesn't stop and wait for you as you grieve. It continues on. A part of you wants desperately to be in that normal flow of life. Another part yells, "Wait a minute. I need a little more time!" It was fortunate I had the luxury of time to grieve. How difficult it must be for those who can't get off the merry-go-round of life long enough to process their feelings.

I believe we do a great injustice to people when we subtly or otherwise demand they "get over it" and move on. Or even indicate to them that they might be feeling sorry for themselves. At some point we do need to continue with life, but grieving takes time and I believe our culture is often insensitive to the utter devastation the death of a loved one has on a person. Instead of demanding they enter the mainstream of life as soon as possible after a loss, we need to be validating and supporting their time of recovery. We give people time to recover from physical injury or surgery. But it seems we deny them the time to recover from emotional injury and loss without paying a huge penalty.

What do you say to a person who is grieving? What words do you use to comfort or ease their pain? Often people are afraid of saying the wrong thing, so they shy away from saying anything so they won't increase the survivor's pain and grief. But the truth is, when people say nothing about the person who has died, it's as though their life before death never existed. Expecting life to resume as usual and avoiding discussion of their loss only increases the pain. Crying is natural and healing. But when people see tears, they often feel they might be making the pain worse. But it is the loss itself that creates the pain and the tears. Talking about the person we loved who has died validates that person's worth to the survivor and helps in the healing. I was grateful I had so many friends who weren't afraid to talk about Le Roy and all the good times we shared. And we grieved together.

My Journal:
Where am I in this grief process? There is a part of me that goes on. Hard realities confront me with hard choices. And these realities have so many layers and levels of "knowing." There is the cold, hard simple truth that can be likened to a piece of wood floating on the water. But as that wood gradually soaks up more and more water, it becomes heavier and heavier and sinks lower and lower.

So it is with reality. As we soak up more and more awareness of what we have lost, we sink to new, deeper levels of emotional understanding. I fear I have many layers of grieving and "knowing" to go through. But for now I just struggle to absorb my new existence on the surface. But when I am pulled down to a new level of awareness, my heart cries out in pain.

There were times when my mind took me back to those last days and I would question whether I had done enough. Did I tell him often enough how much I loved him? Was there anything I could have done differently? That too is a typical response to loss. And I had to remind myself that I did everything humanly possible to make his life as comfortable as I could.

Not everyone who faces a death is able to take solace in remembering happy times. Often there is the "if only…" or "I wish…." and the sadness of what might have been and now could never be becomes another layer of grief. The time has run out and there are no new opportunities to alter the past. At such times it is necessary to come to terms with the reality that there probably would never have been enough time, and we are never able to do all the things we think we might have or should have done in retrospect. We live in an imperfect world. And the task then is to recover from your grief, guilt and anger and sadness by telling yourself firmly that you did all you could with what you had at the time; because that is the truth.

I was so grateful for the good relationship Le Roy and I had. There were no things left unsaid and no regrets. After Le Roy died, I watched as a friend struggled with a marriage that was crumbling, and I thought about the wonderful marriage Le Roy and I shared. We never asked the other to give up his identity or personality to become what we wanted him to be. We encouraged each other to stretch and grow. But our individuality never destroyed our relationship as a couple. We were friends. We liked each other and enjoyed spending time together. Instead of sparring mates, we were a team that together struggled with life's challenges. We gave each other safety within the marriage walls to talk about doubts and fears and uncertainties, and we knew that the other would protect as well as honor that. We not only respected each other, but were loyal to our relationship.

Chapter 12

A Grief so Deep

*G*rowing up in a patriarchal home, there are always remnants of seeing God through the eyes of a child. If you have had a dad who does not show affection or does not know how to comfort or console, and you feel you are always trying to measure up, those same attributes are often unconsciously applied to God.

During those early months of grieving I discovered just how much God loved me. At times when the depth of my loss would overwhelm me, I would find myself curling into a fetal position, crying with an agony so intense no sound was made. I felt like a mortally wounded animal.

And it was there I felt God draw near me as never before, felt Him pick me up in His "spiritual arms," and hold me as only the most loving and caring Father could do. This will forever be what God is to me – my Heavenly Father whose love is so great I can't begin to fathom its depth and enormity. This same love He extends to each and every one of us. It is not anything we earn or deserve. It is a gift – His gift – as was His son Jesus Christ who died for us on the cross.

This was not an insensitive, uncaring, unthinking, unfeeling, or judgmental God. This was a God who wept with me and who cared more than any earthly parent could. And as my journal entries indicated, in the midst of this terrible and at times seemingly unbearable grief, I received not only peace and comfort, but even moments of joy.

As I re-read my journal entries, I marvel at that fact alone, for how could I experience joy in the midst of such pain? But when you journal, you are writing what you are experiencing at the moment – you are not writing for anybody else. And it is the truth of the moment I experienced that I wish to share with others who might be in pain. Simply come – just as you are – to a heavenly Father who will never, ever turn you away – ever! We might turn from Him, but if you come with an honest heart, He will never turn away from you.

Peace. What an amazing phenomenon. The peace that I received from God didn't take me away from the reality of what was happening. But somehow I found myself in a different space emotionally, physically and psychologically. It was more than just a sense of calm, rest and tranquility. The peace that God gave me at those moments when I needed it so desperately seemed to permeate my body and soul and heal the wounds deep inside me. Those moments were islands of refuge in a sea of grief that threatened to engulf and swallow me up.

My Journal:
Yesterday was easier. There was some sun. I started a more positive self-talk to keep me going when I wanted to run away from the office duties at hand. I had tea with Pat in the afternoon, talked with Anita, and saw people and friends. May and Frank and Denny and Joanne came over in the evening and brought dinner. And I slept through the night until seven in the morning.

Friends. It was the love and actions of all my friends that sustained me when Le Roy was ill. And they didn't desert me now either. People would call to see how I was doing. They didn't just ask what they could do. They said they would pick me up to go shopping or just stopped by. It seemed there wasn't a day went by when someone didn't call and say they were having "such and such" for dinner and wanted me to join them. It was an invitation of sincerity and not of duty. And I went.

Even though I didn't feel like socializing, or didn't think I had the energy, some primal urging deep inside said I needed to go, needed the love and laughter and caring of these friends in order to survive. It helped normalize life. It also helped my friends grieve. They, too, had reeled from Le Roy's untimely death.

And I discovered as never before how important it is to continue to reach out to anyone who has suffered a loss. It isn't enough to call and ask if there is something you can do; or to tell a grieving friend to call if they need anything. Because when you are grieving you don't even know what it is you need. Often you feel as though you don't want to intrude with your emotional pain or burden others with it. Sometimes it is just too difficult to put into words what you are experiencing. And there is a fear deep inside that says if you have to ask or rely too much on others you won't be able to make it on your own. And you desperately need to believe you are going to make it. God was my anchor at home – my friends were my lifeline and anchor to the outside world.

I used to be the teacher – teaching my friends and others how to let go. But now, I became the student and they were teaching me about great giving and great loving. And I am reminded today that while only I can walk this walk, they are reaching out to help me on it. Only I can choose to spend quiet time each morning, reflecting and releasing my grief onto paper so it doesn't have such power over me. And only I can choose to allow my friends to support me.

As I struggled with emotions, I tried to focus away from my grief and onto God and ways to initiate healing. Pain, whether physical or emotional, isn't constant even though it might seem that way. It comes and goes like waves, with highs and lows. There were times when the pain seemed so acute I was unable to move, and then there were times when life went on like usual.

The ups and downs of emotions during grief are normal and natural.

Grieving a loss often triggers conflicting emotions and past losses. Sometimes you think you are going crazy. People might feel angry and betrayed by a God they trusted, or feel their loved one was taken too soon. Sometimes we are angry with ourselves for not saying I love you often enough, or we feel guilty for harsh words said when death was unexpected. My loss triggered childhood losses of loneliness. I grew up the youngest in a large family of ten, and often felt I was on the perimeters of family life. How important it is to remember God is perfectly capable of dealing with all our emotions including our anger. He doesn't want us to keep any thoughts or feelings from Him. He wants us to come with an open and honest heart and that means sharing everything with Him – including your doubts and fears and yes, your anger as well. He already knows your heart.

My children were struggling with their grief as well. Aria was so little and required so much attention. Bob was finishing his bachelor's degree program while still working and supporting his family. In the fall he began his Masters of Education program. Don was a free-lance conceptual artist in Los Angeles. Their grieving had to be squeezed in between those demands.

Even my little five-pound Yorkshire terrier, Dickens, suffered from the death of Le Roy. He and Le Roy had been such good buddies. We used to laugh over a silly bedtime play ritual they had. Le Roy would take off his t-shirt and put one of Dickens small toys inside. Dickens would roll and fight with that t-shirt until he had rolled it into a ball. At some point, as he kept working on that shirt, he retrieved his toy and panting hard would hurry over to drop it in front of Le Roy. And they would start all over again. I was not able to continue their ritual.

After Le Roy died, Dickens would lie on his side of the bed with his ears pointed upward – listening – alert to every sound – waiting – waiting for Le Roy to come home. And he would get upset and agitated whenever I wept. He could be asleep in another room, but even if I was crying silently, he seemed to sense my pain. Within a few minutes, he would be frantically jumping on my leg until I picked him up so he could lick away my tears. How could I comfort him when I couldn't comfort myself? He got very sick from infected teeth that summer and I remember thinking, "God, oh God, he can't die too." So many parts of my life seemed to be held together by thin little threads.

Like Dickens, I wonder if somewhere deep inside me, I too was waiting for Le Roy to return. Later that first year I went to the airport to pick up my kids. Because of 9/11 and new tight security laws I had to wait a long way away from where people disembarked from the planes. As I stood there waiting, I suddenly felt as though any moment I would see Le Roy walking down that hallway towards me. It was such a strong and powerful feeling, it literally took my breath away and I struggled to maintain composure. My heart was racing, my breathing became shallow and constricted and I fought to keep from either running away or breaking down completely. If I didn't stay where I was I would miss my kids' arrival. So I dabbed at my eyes and stood very still and prayed until I was able to let go of the intensity of the moment.

There were happy times mixed in with the grieving that first summer. I had friends over for dinner, we celebrated birthdays and we laughed and shared stories of good times together. Tom and Dede had returned from England for the summer. They had always stayed with us on these summer vacations and we joked about their having a permanent bedroom just waiting for them. It was very painful for Tom to walk into the house this time because when he did it really hit that Le Roy was gone. We were expecting to spend the summer together. Because Dede had flown home in February at some level she was more prepared.

Aria's baptism had been delayed not only because of her grandfather's death, but also because her dad's work took him away from home for several weeks. On July 1st, friends, family and godparents all gathered at our church for her baptism. What a joyful event it was. Pastor Kevin invited all friends and family to gather around the baptismal font during the baptism. There were so many people it was difficult to find space for everyone. Aria looked beautiful in her new baptismal dress. I had started sewing it before Le Roy got sick and it had been a healing project to finish after he died. We all felt Le Roy's presence.

Everyone came to our house after the service for food and a continuation of the celebration. The house was full of people; it was a warm sunny day and we were able to spend time on the large deck that looked out over Shelter Bay and La Conner. Gifts were given and speeches made. I gave Aria one of the violins Le Roy's dad had owned along with the sheet music to a piano piece Le Roy liked to play when he was taking piano lessons as a child – "Claire de Lune." Despite the sadness that lurked in the background, we laughed and enjoyed the moment together.

There were other meaningful events that summer as well. The musicians in Portland held a "wake" for Le Roy and another much-respected and loved musician who had died. It was overwhelming to see all those professional musicians come to play in honor of them. Less than a month after Le Roy died, our oldest son graduated with his BA degree. I knew Le Roy was there watching with pride as Bob walked up to receive his diploma. Two years later he would graduate with his Master's degree in teaching, following in his dad's footsteps.

Chapter 13

Music and More Music

Le Roy had been a professional musician as well as a college teacher and chairman of the music department of Clackamas Community College. Before I met him he traveled with big bands who played the music of the 40's; Glen Miller's band under Tex Beneke, Charlie Spivak, Buddy Morrow and Charlie Barnet. He played at the Palladium in Hollywood and played in the relief band at the Sands hotel in Las Vegas for such stars as Lena Horne and Sammy Davis, Jr. A musician had to be very accomplished in order to play in the relief band. The level of expertise required meant you did not need lots of rehearsal time to play the special music for each show and could step in for the regular bands with little notice.

I met him shortly after he returned from Las Vegas to his home town of Portland, Oregon to live. After we were married, he started putting together music to form his own band and over the years put together music for four different size bands; from eight pieces to seventeen. The music was the sounds of the big bands still popular long after the 40's and 50's. He booked all four of his bands over the years throughout the northwest and people loved to dance to his bands.

He didn't just play jazz, but played with the Oregon Symphony and the Oregon Symphonic Pops, and directed a house band at the Hoyt Hotel in Portland, five nights a week, for seven years. When Broadway shows, ice shows, circuses and name performers came to

Portland, Le Roy was always hired to be a part of the band. One of my special memories was sitting quietly beside him in the covered orchestra pit one night, as he played the Broadway show, "Chorus Line," for its second run through Portland. Since the pit was covered and he knew the music, Le Roy brought one or two select students from the college to sit quietly beside him while he played so they could experience what it was like to play a Broadway show. One night I became one of those students.

His playing was so versatile that later in life he was asked to travel with and direct one of the Zirbini's circus groups for a short period of time. Playing circus music is very demanding and exhausting. Directing it is even more challenging. Timing is crucial to each act's performance. I took a leave of absence from my graduate studies to travel with him that year. It was a great adventure, and I'll never forget the time in Canada where we were doing one night stands. Every afternoon when the circus arrived in a new town, the huge circus tent was put up and after the show it was taken down. Everyone traveling with the circus was parked close together as these one night stands were at shopping malls in small towns. One night the huge trailer carrying the elephants was parked next to us and when I opened the door of our RV in the morning, ten feet away from me the elephants were getting their morning bath, scrubbed by their trainers using huge brushes with handles. How many people get an experience like that? Our kids, who were grown at the time, loved to tell their friends their parents had run away with the circus.

Over the years Le Roy had accumulated a lot of music. A lot of it was organized and categorized, but a lot was not. There were boxes and filing cabinets full of instrumental music, both classical and jazz, music for quartets and trios and solos and duets, and yes even some circus music he had arranged. There were instructional and teaching books. It had to be inventoried in order for me to sell or donate it.

That summer after he died it was a comfort to immerse myself in his music. A friend and colleague of Le Roy's came up from Portland several times to help, but there was so much music it seemed to only make a dent. But it wasn't just the physical music I was immersed in, but all the wonderful memories attached to it. For I loved to listen to Le Roy play his trombone, and like other band wives, would come to dance jobs and concerts to listen and be a part of our husbands' musical world. It was our world too.

Almost prophetically the Christmas before Le Roy died he told our oldest son that if anything happened to him, "Tell Mom not to just give away all the music, because it has a lot of value." So I made it my mission to be sure his music lived on. I was determined to honor his life by doing this. But it was an awesome and at times very daunting and formidable task and one that took over two years to complete. After a year, my oldest son asked me if I was going to spend the rest of my life working on Dad's music. He said to me, "Dad wouldn't want you to do that." But what I was doing was my own labor of love and I needed to do that for me as well as for any memories.

Over the years of playing dance jobs and concerts, Le Roy had taped some of his live performances. He was an excellent bandleader and director as well as trombone player. I found it a great comfort to listen to these tapes that summer, hearing him play his trombone, hearing his voice and listening to his music and even seeing him on some videotapes. He was still here with me through his music and recordings.

It was during these first few months that I experienced visits from Le Roy. Oh, I didn't see him; but I felt his presence as if he were there beside me, and with eyes closed I saw him in my mind as clear as day. I could internally hear his voice and I would answer without a word being spoken. I had heard of such phenomena occurring, but I was unprepared for the truly incredible and unexpected experience it was.

The first time this occurred was when I was listening to one of those dance band live performance tapes. As he played a trombone solo, I physically "felt" his arms around me and we were dancing. In a goodbye letter to him, I wrote:

"I found all the tapes of your dance bands over the years and have been listening to them. Tonight as I listened to a recording of a Valentine's Day dance you played with your twelve-piece band years ago, I started crying. I was transported back to that night and as I closed my eyes, I could see the band and the people dancing and

you playing your trombone. You played so sweetly! And suddenly I found myself in your arms! You were dancing with me! I asked how you could play your horn and dance with me at the same time and you said, "I can do that now!" You danced divinely. You did not have any trouble dancing. It was wonderful! With my eyes closed, I not only could hear you play, but could 'see' and 'feel' your arms around me as we danced."

Because he was always playing, we seldom had an opportunity to dance. He was a lousy dancer and didn't really enjoy dancing that much. But every once in awhile he would come down off the bandstand and dance a dance with me. Those were special moments, as I loved to dance. After he retired from teaching and we moved to Washington, we took ball room dancing lessons because he knew how much I loved to dance and he tried to improve. He was better directing the band!

I had several other visits from Le Roy. Another time was early in the morning during my quiet time with God and writing. In that visit Le Roy and I had this internal conversation about our love and marriage. He told me to trust my inner instincts and that God was with me.

As a counselor I have a scientific background in psychology. As a Christian and student of God's word, I realize there are many things that are unexplainable by science and there is much about the spiritual realm we do not understand or comprehend. These were very real experiences I had. This was a spiritual connection that occurred as surely as if Le Roy was standing in the room. I described it in my journal this way:

It's like I feel a physical presence, but it is only a spiritual one. It's as though God has given me 'spiritual' ears to hear and feel Le Roy. How do I know I am not just creating it – wishing he were here with me? I don't know. But I do know the visits are totally unexpected and surprise me. I have no control over when it happens. I experience calm and peace.

The last thing I needed to do that summer was inter Le Roy's ashes. It took a couple of months to organize everything. Finally on July 23rd, a small group of friends and family gathered at Willamette Memorial Cemetery in Portland, Oregon for a final goodbye. Le Roy was born in Portland and grew up there and his family along with my mom and dad were buried in the cemetery that bordered the national veteran's cemetery. Pastor Kevin made the four and a half hour drive to preside over the small service we held in the outdoor chapel.

Once again, Le Roy decided to show up. I recorded the experience in my journal.

"Today we took your ashes back to Portland, Le Roy, and laid them to rest at Willamette Memorial. What a beautiful place it is. You made me laugh through my tears. As Pastor Kevin was praying over your ashes during the service, I heard you say, 'You may leave my ashes here, but I'm going home with you!' God, how like you it sounded! Pomp and ceremony are okay, but let's just go home together.

After the outdoor chapel service, we had to drive to the Columbarium where your ashes were placed inside the little niche. I had written you a letter and it is placed in there beside you. I put my hand on the marble with Pastor Kevin as he prayed. But although the tears were flowing, I could sense you were not in those ashes – in fact your spirit was so close to me I could hardly concentrate on the prayer. What was it you were saying to me? 'Those are just ashes – it is not me – I'm here with you.'

I had asked Earl to play Taps and he had tears in his eyes as he talked about the passing of his beloved wife a year ago. She also was buried at Willamette as Earl, too, was a veteran. He would not accept any money. He wasn't offended – he understood my offering – but he wanted to do this as a gift to you. Gary overheard our conversation and said, "We musicians have so little to give – only our music." I was deeply touched. Earl played Taps beautifully. I wanted somehow to reach out and comfort both Gary and Earl as they lost someone they loved, respected and honored deeply when you died." [Earl and Gary were friends and colleagues of Le Roy.]

Le Roy, your ashes are home – but please stay with me in spirit as long as I need you. We love you – I love you. While I still feel your presence at times, I grieve the loss of your physical being. I want to put arms around you physically. But I can only touch you spiritually. How is it a person can cry and laugh at the same time?"

That was the last time I felt or sensed Le Roy "speak" to me. He "spoke" to one other person besides me that day. That same evening, two of our long-time friends, Jack and Iva Sue, were attending the dedication of the new "Oregon Gardens" in Silverton, Oregon with the Tommy Dorsey Band. Jack had played drums in Le Roy's band when they played every night at the Hoyt Hotel and for other dance jobs as well. Before the band started playing and while Iva Sue had left her seat for a few minutes, Jack had a "visit" from Le Roy. This is the e-mail I received after I returned home:

Iva went out for some coffee and the band began to play "Marie" and I'll swear to **GOD** *that Le Roy said to me,* ***"IT'S ALL O.K. NOW!"*** *You could have blown me away! I don't think I've ever had that kind of experience before!*

It would be just like Le Roy to go to a big band performance while I stayed at the hotel resting from an emotional day. Why he chose to speak to Jack that day, we don't know. We just know it was a very real experience and one of those moments you simply accept because you cannot explain it. But you know it is as real as the sun in the sky and the music you hear when the band plays.

When I returned home the following day, I felt a healing peace I hadn't experienced since he died. It was as if things were now in place. Did Le Roy come home with me? I never again had the same "spiritual" visits from him, but somehow I knew he was there. There was a sense of him deep inside me, and there were one or two times later when I heard him "speak" to me briefly in my mind – always when I least expected it. But he was never as near or as close as this last visit from him at the cemetery.

Chapter 14

Memories

Many of my journal entries that first year were letters to Le Roy. And often while I was writing I could feel his presence so strongly it was as if I were having a conversation with him in person. Somehow, it was important to identify and put down on paper all the things I had gained from our relationship, for they were special gifts to me as I began to think of myself as a single person.

My Journal:
Thank you Le Roy for all the years of faithfulness and love – your concern for me financially and yes, I am taken care of.

Thank you for teaching me to take time before making decisions – to think things through carefully – to play devil's advocate – to look for loopholes – to ask questions. Thank you for teaching me to love traveling, to accept people for who they are instead of judging them. Thank you for your wisdom and sense of humor. You taught me how to laugh at myself and my world, often when I didn't want to. You taught me to love myself and you didn't like it when I put myself down. You taught me that the best wasn't necessarily the most expensive, that being frugal wasn't simply accepting the cheapest or least. You taught me to live in the here and now, to rest and not push myself. I think I can go on now, and will take your love and gifts with me and expand them. I miss you so much.

I would bask in those warm memories. But almost as quickly, I would remember how much I had lost. And I struggled with letting go.

My Journal:
God, Oh God, I miss him. Yes I am moving on, but I miss that sense of belonging just to him – knowing that he would always be there – loyal, stable. He wouldn't get shaken. No matter what disaster or crisis we faced, we faced it together. We figured out a way to deal with it and move on. Now I must learn how to face this reality alone and figure out how to move on.

"Do not be anxious about anything, but in everything by prayer and petition, with Thanksgiving, present your requests to God. And the peace of God, which transcends all understanding, will guard your hearts and your minds in Christ Jesus." (Phil. 4:6-7)

Grieving gives us an opportunity to reflect on all the good things that have happened and are happening. Without acknowledging the blessings of the past and present, you can get mired in the muck of pain and loss and depression and feel there is nothing left to live for. This is not putting on a Pollyanna happy face and pretending everything is just grand when it isn't. This isn't about running from, or stuffing deep inside or pushing away the grief. It's about taking time to balance your grief with gratefulness and thankfulness is important in the healing process. So I began to write about all the happy times.

Loss can color memories. Remembering the good times doesn't mean you idealize the person into someone that didn't really exist. We had our moments when we got angry with each other. Somehow we instinctively knew that if we said hurtful things that it would hurt ourselves as well. When we were angry or upset or disappointed, we would retreat and wait for the other to say he was sorry. I can remember the struggle between hanging on to my being right and wanting to get back together again; at some point, being apart hurt worse than being right. And about the time I found myself turning towards him, he was turning towards me. At those moments we knew that our relationship was more important than any disagreement, misunderstanding or differences of opinion. It was when we drew together that we could have a discussion. But often, the subject in question had become so irrelevant, little discussion was necessary.

As I went through pictures and memories, there had been so many good times: the year we spent in England working; the places we visited; running away with the circus; designing and building our dream house in Shelter Bay; the boating trips in the San Juan and Gulf Islands; camping with our kids; the birth of our grandchildren to name a few. Were there any special ones that stood out? Each one seemed important.

When Le Roy returned to Portland from Las Vegas it was to move home for good. A blind date set up by a mutual friend brought us together shortly after his return and a year later we were married. I continued working as a legal secretary and he started selling real estate and played dance jobs. One of his real estate commissions was used as a down payment for our first home.

But real estate wasn't enough to pay the bills. Our first baby, Bob, required a hernia operation at three months, and we did not have health insurance. So after getting a temporary teaching certificate to teach music in the grade schools, Le Roy enrolled in a Masters of Music Education program. He started playing with the symphony and played dance jobs on week ends to earn the extra money it took for us to live and move forward.

Those early years in that tiny house were full of ups and downs. Le Roy's parents' marriage ended in divorce and we brought his mom home to live with us for a while as she had heart problems. Elizabeth was born eighteen months after Bob, and five years later our last son, Don, was born. He was a big baby – ten pounds – and looked like a little football player. But after six months and still unable to hold up his head, our pediatrician sent us to a specialist. This observant and careful physician believed Don was missing some neck muscles, and both doctors felt that he could be tested and given a better evaluation at the Oregon Medical School Hospital in Portland.

After a week of testing we were told he had cerebral palsy and we should get a brace made for him as soon as possible so he could learn to walk. It turned out he did not have cerebral palsy, but was missing neck muscles. I think it was hard to evaluate him because while he was a happy baby at home, at the hospital I was told he cried most of the time. At that time they didn't allow parents to spend time at the hospital except during visiting hours. I was thankful that it didn't have a lasting effect on him and when we brought him home he reverted to his happy playful self. He not only learned to walk in his brace, but did the usual boy things such as swinging on ropes, playing on drums and he even learned to play trombone. He was in cub scouts and loved to act. Wearing the brace never stopped him. He started drawing as soon as he could hold a pencil and today is a creative artist working in many different mediums. With the three children, and one of them in a brace, it was a full time and challenging job to keep everything together. During those years, Le Roy worked nights as well as teaching during the day.

It didn't take long before we outgrew our home and built a new and larger one. Le Roy started teaching at Clackamas Community College and was chairman of the Music Department for over thirty years. Many of his students went on to play professionally, either part time or full time. Some became music teachers. One became a successful composer in Los Angeles. Le Roy never wanted to become a teacher, but he was an excellent one and many students looked up to him, not only as a teacher and professional musician, but as a mentor and father figure. He was highly respected for the principles and values by which he lived his life. Three years after his death he was honored at the school where he taught for so many years. With the construction of a new music, theatre arts building, a special dedication was held in his honor before the building was officially dedicated. Over 125 people attended for the sit down catered meal, video presentation of his life and dancing afterwards to his 17 piece band made up of former students and colleagues. The music rehearsal hall was named after him.

Even though we both led very busy lives, we somehow managed to take time out for ourselves even if that just meant a quick trip to beautiful Victoria, Canada once a year. Often a night out meant going with him to one of his dance jobs. Although there were times I wished we could have had more quiet dinners out by ourselves, I really enjoyed going to dance jobs with him. I loved listening to the music and visiting with the musicians at intermission. Sometimes other band wives would be there. Whenever a Broadway show came to town and he was hired to play in the band, he would always get me a ticket to see the show. I got to see many Broadway shows and performances that I would never have seen if he weren't playing.

We bought a tent and took the kids camping in the summer time. When the kids were older we bought a sailboat and spent weekends sailing and cruising. After all our children were in school, I returned to college and eventually got my masters degree in psychology and counseling and I began teaching at Clackamas Community College as well.

Although the years were busy and sometimes extremely stressful, they still were good years, full of wonderful memories and special times together. Le Roy always enjoyed having me with him whenever possible, and I made a decision early in our marriage to be available, especially after the children were older. So I was a part of his life and work.

When he wasn't working and was home, he was such a patient and loving dad. When the kids were little, he would lie on the floor and they would have a ball wrestling with him. They sat beside him in his big chair and read him their stories and showed him their art work. He would take them with him when he had to run errands. We went together as a family to church and sometimes on simple day trips and outings. Somewhere in his busy schedule he found time to be at almost all the school functions and performances. And as they got older, he calmly listened to their problems and helped them make decisions.

Wonderful memories! "I love you, Le Roy. And we miss you so very much."

Chapter 15

Another Crisis - Another Struggle

How interesting the grief process was that first year - the twists and turns it took. It was a time of letting go and still hanging on. I was trying to fit into a new skin. Who was I now? How would I create meaning in my life again? At times it felt I was moving forward, discovering a new path I could take, and then it was as though I had been going in a circle and had returned to the same spot again.

My Journal:
Monday I felt as though I was emerging from a fog - a bad dream - a long nightmare. And suddenly I wanted to live. For several months I had experienced a subtle depression – a feeling of not wanting to go on. I wasn't suicidal, just feeling there wasn't really anything to live for.

Depression. It drops over me at times like a net – a web that snares me – or a fog I can't touch or see but which colors my world gray. It sneaks up on me and steals my desire to go on.

But those times were fleeting and at some point life became more than just tolerable. I was healing and knew I could not only live without Le Roy but could create a new life without him that did not mean forgetting him.

Recovery was more than just healing. It was also a discovery process of who I was as a single person. So many years had been spent as a couple. It wasn't easy making that transition from "we" to "I." The fear of the unknown was gradually being replaced with the anticipation of new beginnings. I was stronger, wiser and more competent than I had felt in those early days of loss. I was comfortable in my own skin and accepted both my strengths and my weaknesses. Writing was not so much therapy but a way to express thoughts and feelings creatively. I was moving on and in the process was writing my story.

My morning study and writing time gave me the opportunity to learn more about my God. Although I had taught Sunday school for years and had developed some of the curriculum I used, I was discovering at a new level just how deeply God loves His people. As I studied my Bible again, from beginning to end, I saw with fresh insight, that the people in those Bible stories were just like you and me. They doubted and struggled to believe and make sense of what was happening to them. They often did not understand or comprehend how God was working in their lives. He was not a God "up there," but a God who was in the very trenches of our lives. He was there with us in the dirty business of living where doubts and fears existed. My relationship with Him was more than just reading scripture. It was bringing everything to Him every day and He met me there – every day. He was faithful – even when I was not.

I read and re-read the book of Job. I could identify with Job's struggles to believe. Like Job, I realized that not only did God love me, but He was with me night and day. I would never truly be alone as long as I was willing to let Him remain in my life. His love for each of us far exceeds our expectations or understanding.

And then crisis struck again!

A few months before the first anniversary of Le Roy's death, my daughter Elizabeth discovered a lump in her breast. She was still nursing Aria and everyone thought the lump was simply an infected or engorged milk duct. But her doctors were diligent. A biopsy revealed an aggressive cancerous growth still in its infancy.

The news was like a wrecking ball flying through the air knocking all of us flat. My world came to a halt once again. "Why

God? Why? Please don't take her too. Aria is only fourteen months old. She needs her Mom." I remember telling God I rather He took me because I had already lived a full life, and Aria needed her mom. I wasn't trying to be a martyr. I meant it.

My first reaction was shock and disbelief. Were you testing our faith, God? But God isn't a God who asks for sacrifices. He wasn't asking me to give up another person I loved. I remember my pastor telling me it was okay to be angry with God. But it was too exhausting to be angry.

It took a day or two to stabilize my thinking. God is a God of love. He is not an ogre who manipulates people or tests them to see whether they love Him. He doesn't ask them to become sacrifices. God doesn't need our sacrifices. Elizabeth got cancer because we live in a fallen world. Her late-in-life pregnancy and all the hormonal activity associated with it, as well as the stress of a premature baby and losing her father might all have contributed to it. We don't know.

The tumor was discovered just before Elizabeth and her husband were ready to move into a new and larger home. The day after they moved, Elizabeth went into surgery. The lump was removed and the surrounding tissue showed no cancer cells. The prognosis was excellent. To reduce the risk of its return, however, my daughter chose to go through six months of chemotherapy and seven weeks of radiation.

All the things I had started to do along with my new outlook on life came to a halt during this time as my energy went to helping my daughter, helping care for Aria and helping in the home in whatever way I could. Elizabeth would be on chemo for two weeks and then off a week. After her initial chemo drip at the beginning of each third week, she would get very sick but she had a fighting spirit and positive attitude. In the middle of her pain she worked hard to hide her great discomfort from her little daughter and those around her. She was a tower of strength for all of us.

After spending two or three days at her house, I would come home for a few days and then return again. When I came home, I worked hard to keep my potted plants watered and blooming, for their beauty lifted my spirits. When the weather was real hot, I once again relied on my friends to help me.

My Journal:
I feel like I'm on a battlefield - a minefield - with craters all around. No sooner do I crawl out of one crater then I seem to fall into another. It's getting harder to crawl out of them because I am getting more and more tired. I feel exhausted and it is taking longer to recover. I thought my journey through the minefields was over. But now it seems I am back on that battlefield.

And now another hit: My pain levels are increasing. My hip and back have been bothering me. I hope I won't need any more surgery. But the pain is draining me of any reserve energy I have left.

My lower back was fused and now my left hip and lower back were hurting more and more. When I got rear ended that summer at a stop light, therapy was worked into the schedule. It seems my psyche was still more fragile than I knew and with the increased physical pain levels it was difficult to keep a positive outlook. I'd cry at the drop of a hat. My prayers were pleas for God to give all of us the physical and emotional strength to be able to continue helping my daughter. I was beginning to feel like a broken vessel being crushed and ground to bits.

My Journal:
Am I feeling sorry for myself? I would like to think I'm not, because I don't like to feel this way. I hate it. I want to feel confident – not hopeless. But it seems whenever I climb out of a new hole, I'm knocked back into it, and the reserves needed to get up again are diminishing.

I decided I needed to do more. I yelled out loud to myself: **"ENOUGH!** *It's time to walk out of this minefield. I am going to take my life back! I will visualize good things happening. I can do this. I have many friends and a support system that doesn't end. It's up to me to discover ways to move ahead. I can and I will!"* And it was a mantra I kept repeating throughout that next year.

By Christmas of that year, Elizabeth's prognosis was positive and things began to return to normal. In January, I continued my inventory of Le Roy's music. As I typed music titles into my computer, I recorded all of our large LP collection of big band music onto CDs. I ended up with over fifty CDs. While listening to the music images of Le Roy playing in the bands brought tears to my eyes and my grieving resumed.

My Journal:
I think about Le Roy and how well he played: the look of contentment and satisfaction he had when he played with a big band. And I remembered all those dances I went to with him and watched as he played. As I listen, I am connected again to the past. I miss him. I miss those times so very much.

Will I ever stop weeping? My days are busy with projects and doing things. I put on the happy face, and yet it seems the emptiness remains and I struggle to keep moving forward. Le Roy and our marriage had meant so much to me. I know it is possible to have a new life - meet another man - fall in love again, but I don't know how to get from here to there. I keep trying. But the road map keeps taking me on detours.

To love greatly means you will experience grief deeply. I loved Le Roy greatly. The pain of grief seemed at times unending.

Chapter 16

Emerging from the Valley

*G*rieving, like any change, can become an opportunity for discovery. Through my journaling I discovered I not only enjoyed writing, but others seemed to enjoy reading what I had written. My journals, my time with God, had fed my soul, and I was encouraged to share my journey and what I had learned with others.

Part of grieving and recovering from my loss was discovering a new purpose and meaning for my life. Only when I gave myself permission to see that new experiences held the potential to be as meaningful as my past, could I begin to move forward. Although I was able to let go and grieve fully the loss of Le Roy, there were moments when it was still hard to move forward. It was only when I was willing to give God my entire future as well as my life that I walked out of that valley of shadows for good.

Loss is a profound injury and to heal from those wounds to the heart and spirit, we need to give ourselves time and permission to mourn and grieve. We talk about having hearts that are tender and loving. Yet, when those hearts are wounded we treat them as though they were tough shoe leather. Tears and pain can still be triggered easily. The healing of the heart and psyche takes longer than we expect, and it seems my soul and spirit and emotional system have been forever altered to the sensitivity of pain around me.

People have said, "You'll get over" your loss. But I don't believe we get over our losses. I believe they become woven into the fabric of our lives. And in the integration and recovery process we become stronger individuals. It's like bones that heal. They become stronger than before they were broken. There always remains a sadness of what we lost or what can never be, but over time it no longer drains us of our energy and we can move forward in life.

It has been six years since Le Roy died. As a single woman, I not only have survived my loss, but have gone on to re-claim and re-create a new life. I resumed singing, taking voice lessons to improve my voice. I have sold and built a new home and traveled. I have entertained, made new friends and strengthened the relationships of old friends. I have accepted leadership positions both within the community and within my church and have written an on-line ADHD Parenting course. I continue to expand my writing and am currently compiling snippets of my journal into a new book. I have been blessed by God and feel His blessings and presence with me every day.

There are still times early in the morning hours when I weep for what I no longer have. But I know God is working out the details of my future and I have become stronger in so many ways. My faith and belief in God has grown into a more profound and personal relationship with my heavenly Father and Lord. I come to Him now because I want to not because I believe I "should," "must" or "have to." I come to Him not just because He is God, awesome and mighty, but because He truly is my Heavenly Father, Savior, Lord and my friend.

As I develop the talents and abilities God has given me, I allow my weaknesses to be an opportunity and challenge to grow. My life has taken on a new richness and depth of meaning. Love continues to be the most important and dominant theme in my life and I find myself drawn to share God's love with others – especially those who are in pain.

We will experience losses every day. Some will be "paper cuts," some bruises, and some deep internal wounds. Some losses will be the passing from one season of our life to another. Some will be tragedies that will be difficult to talk openly about, such as the loss of a childhood due to physical, emotional or sexual abuse, or the tragedy of a family member going to prison. Sometimes the losses may seem insignificant, such as retirement, or the loss of a pet to a child. But all losses require grieving. To minimize any loss is to deny ourselves the ability to grow.

The author of Ecclesiastes wrote so many, many years ago: "For everything there is a season, and a time for every matter under heaven: a time to be born and a time to die. . . A time to weep, and a time to laugh; a time to mourn, and a time to dance. . ."

This has been a time for me to retreat to find meaning again in the depth of my being and soul. It has been a time to reflect, to be grateful for all I've had and have been given, a time to cut my losses, let go and rest. Without my loss, I would not have gained such a deep level of trust and depth of faith, or be able to experience the love of God as I do today. I would not have learned how to talk so personally and openly with My God and to hear His quiet voice in return. My life has been blessed by it.

As a society we need to reach out to others, to listen, suspend judgment and advice and instead extend understanding, warmth, friendship and support. We can all be an "angel" to someone in need. Each one of us can take a moment to listen and validate. Each one of us can be a part of the healing journey for another; to do less than that is to diminish our humanity.

Printed in the United States
86671LV00005B/313-372/A